HAMSTERLOPAEDIA

A Complete Guide To Hamster Care

Chris and Peter Logsdail &
Kate Hovers BVSc CertSHP MRCVS

D1634333

RINGPRESS

ACKNOWLEDGEMENTS

The publisher would like to thank Keith Allison for the photography featured in the book, and Jonathan Wright (Paws for Thought Pet Centres) for allowing the animals in his care to be photographed. Additional photographs by Rosie Ray.

ABOUT THE AUTHORS

Chris and Peter Logsdail began showing hamsters in 1985. In 1997 and 2000, they won the *Exhibitor of the Year* competition – the highlights in an exhibition career that has seen them reach the Top Ten every year they have entered. Today, Chris and Peter play prominent roles in the hamster fancy, at both club and national level.

Kate Hovers BVSc MRCVS is a qualified vet with expert knowledge of hamsters. Kate has successfully performed many surgical procedures on hamsters – including a Caesarean section.

Published by Ringpress Books,
A Division of Interpet Publishing
Vincent Lane, Dorking, Surrey RH4 3YX

ISBN 1 86054 246 8

Manufactured in Singapore

10 9 8 7 6 5 4 3 2 1

CONTENTS

Page

SECTION ONE: PRINCIPLES OF HAMSTER KEEPING   6
By Chris and Peter Logsdail

1. THE HISTORY OF THE HAMSTER   6
Introducing hamsters; (Species); The European hamster; The
Syrian hamster (Discovery; Classification; Captive Syrians; The
pet market; Physical features); The Chinese hamster
(Discovery and classification; The pet market; Physical
features); Dwarf Russian hamsters (The Winter White; The
Campbell; The Roborovski).

2. CHOOSING A HAMSTER   14
Responsibilities; Possible problems; Hamster appeal (Curiosity;
Endearing eyes; Versatile feet; Cheek pouches); Hamster varieties
(Syrian; Chinese; Campbell; Winter White; Roborovski); Hamster
sources; Sexing (Syrian; Roborovski; Chinese/Other Dwarf species);
Health; Taking home your hamster.

3. HOUSING YOUR HAMSTER   24
Wire-top cages (Design faults); Plastic-tank cages (Problems;
Positioning); Glass-tank cages (Converted aquariums); Laboratory
cages; Homemade cages (Wooden cages; Temporary homemade
cages); Choosing the right cage; Setting up home (Positioning
the cage; Shavings; Bedding material; Water bottles; Food
dishes; Accessories).

4. FEEDING YOUR HAMSTER   33
Pre-mixed foods (Safety first; Changing the mix; Storage); Fresh
foods (Fresh fruit and vegetables; Wild greens); Treats (Simple treats;
Seed treats); High-protein foods; Mashes and milky foods (Teeth and
gums; Suitable foods; How much?); Feeding guidelines (Quantities;
Faddy eaters; After cleaning).

5. CARING FOR YOUR HAMSTER   40
Handling (Biting; The two-handed pick-up; Gaining confidence;
The one-handed pick-up; Dwarf hamsters; Children); Cage
Cleaning (Health checks); Grooming (Longhaired hamsters;
Bathing); Exercise and fun (Exercise balls; Play boxes);
Holidays (Short breaks; Longer holidays); Escape and capture
(Door catches; Modular cages; Catching your hamster).

6. COMMON PROBLEMS 58

Bar rub; Colds; Cuts; Dehydration; Dry ears; Dry skin; Eye problems (Blindness; Entropion; Foreign bodies; 'Gummy' eyes; Loss of an eye); Falls; Hibernation; Hip spots; Kinked tails; Lumps and bumps (Testicular lumps; Mammary lumps; Facial lumps; Dwarf hamsters; Other lumps); Nails; Noises; Scent glands; Strokes; Teeth problems (Overlong teeth; Broken or lost teeth); Thinning fur; Twirling; Urine changes; Weight loss.

SECTION TWO: HEALTH CARE 66
By Kate Hovers BVSc, Cert SHP, MRCVS

7. ANATOMY AND PHYSIOLOGY 66
General information; The skeleton (Skull and jaws; Spine and tail; Limbs); The sense organs (The mouth; The eyes; The ears; The nose; The skin).

8. MAJOR BODY SYSTEMS 72
Respiratory system (Upper respiratory system; Lower respiratory system); Cardiovascular system (Blood; Heart problems); Digestive system (Mouth; Stomach; Small intestine; Large intestine); Endocrine system (Thyroid gland; Parathyroid glands; Adrenal glands; Pituitary gland); Urinary system (Urinary system problems); Reproductive system (Female; Male).

9. A-Z OF HAMSTER DISEASES AND HEALTH PROBLEMS 83
Abscess; Acariasis; Aggression; Allergy; Alopecia; Amputation; Amyloidosis; Anorexia; Baldness; Behavioural problems; Bladder problems; Blindness; Bronchitis; Cage paralysis; Cancer; Cannibalism; Caries; Castration; Cataracts; Collapse; Conjunctivitis; Constipation and impaction; Coprophagy; Corneal ulcer; Cryptorchidism; Cushing's disease; Cystitis; Deafness; Demodex; Diabetes; Diarrhoea; Dislocation; Dystocia; Ear mites; Eclampsia; Eczema; Entropion; Everted cheek pouches; Eye prolapse; False pregnancy; First aid; Fits; Fleas; Foot and mouth disease; Fractures; Glaucoma; Haematuria; Hamster plague; Head tilt; Heart disease; Heat stroke; Hibernation; Hind limb paralysis; Hypothyroidism; Impacted cheek pouches; Impaction; Infertility; Intussusception; Kidney disease; Liver disease; Lymphocytic choriomeningitis virus (LCMV); Malocclusion; Mammary tumours; Mange; Mastitis; Microphthalmia; Obesity; Orchitis; Ovarian cysts; Ovariohysterectomy; Overgrown toenails; Papova virus; Paralysis; Pneumonia; Polycystic disease; Polyuria and polydipsia; Pseudopregnancy; Pyometra; Rabies; Rectal prolapse; Respiratory infection; Ringworm; Salmonellosis;

4

Sarcoptic mange; Satinisation; Scurf; Skin sores; Spaying; Stillbirth; Stroke; Teeth; Testicular cancer; Tumours/neoplasia; Tyzzer's disease; Urolithiasis; Vitamin deficiencies; Warts; Weight loss; Wet tail; Worms; Wounds; Yersinia; Zoonosis.

SECTION THREE: BREEDING AND SHOWING 111
By Chris and Peter Logsdail

10. BREEDING SYRIAN HAMSTERS 111
The breeding pair (Female; Male; Pairings to avoid); Mating (Introducing the pair; Mating; Mating problems); Pregnancy and birth; The nursing mother (Covering babies; Infanticide; Mothering instinct); The babies (7 to 14 days; 14 to 21 days; 21 days onwards); Separating mother and babies (Running on); Fostering and hand-rearing (Fostering; Hand-rearing); Record keeping; Colours and patterns (Terminology; Colours and patterns; Coat types); Simple genetics (Genetic terms); Colour combinations (Natural colour mutations; Two-colour combinations; Three-colour combinations; Four-colour combinations; Principles of colour breeding).

11. BREEDING CHINESE AND DWARF HAMSTERS 146
Breeding Chinese (Colonies; Mixed pairs; Pairings/colonies to avoid; Pregnancy; Birth; The babies; Separating parents and babies); A note before breeding Dwarfs; Breeding Campbells (Pairings to avoid; Mating; Pregnancy; Birth; The babies; Separating parents and babies); Breeding Winter Whites (The breeding pair; Pairings to avoid; Mating; Pregnancy and birth; The babies); Breeding Roborovskis (Mixed pairs; Pairings to avoid; Pregnancy and birth; The babies); Fostering and hand-rearing; Record keeping; Colours and patterns (Terminology; Campbell colours and patterns; Campbell coat types; Winter White colours and patterns; Chinese colours and patterns; Roborovski colours and patterns); Simple genetics; Colour combinations (Chinese; Campbell; Winter White; Roborovski).

12. SHOWING YOUR HAMSTER 161
Joining a club; Showing for beginners; Show structure; The Pet section (Judging); The Syrian section (Classes; First-time entrants; Presentation; Judging); The Dwarf (or Other Species) section (More than one?; Judging).

APPENDICES 170
1. Useful contacts 170
2. Websites 173

CHAPTER 1

THE HISTORY OF THE HAMSTER

1. Introducing hamsters
2. The European hamster
3. The Syrian hamster
4. The Chinese hamster
5. Dwarf Russian hamster

The hamster is among the most popular of pets, and given the comparatively short time this small animal has been known in the western world, its popularity and geographical spread is phenomenal.

Despite being the butt of many jokes, hamsters are very much beloved by their owners, both young and old. Hamsters are scrupulously clean, they do not have exotic dietary requirements so are relatively cheap to feed, and they can be kept almost anywhere in the house or a small flat. Indeed, they are most accommodating pets.

1. INTRODUCING HAMSTERS

The word 'hamster' comes from the German word 'hamstern', meaning to hoard. Hoarding is a characteristic of all hamsters, captive or wild, and it is a reflection of their diet and the lands in which each species originated. Harsh, cold weather conditions, or long periods of drought, means that a 'hoard' of food is a necessity to survive as an individual or as a colony. A  characteristic of most species is the cheek pouch, which enables them to transport the 'hoard' back to their abode.

Most hamsters have a short tail (almost a bob-tail) and short legs, characteristics usually found in animals that spend most of their active life underground. Hamsters are not strictly subterranean – they forage above ground for food – but a significant amount of their time is spent underground in daylight hours, to avoid predators, the daytime heat, or the extreme cold of winter. The hamster's short-but-powerful legs are excellent for burrowing and pushing out the loosened soil, as anyone who has witnessed a pet hamster ridding its cage of shavings can testify.

As with many small rodents, the life expectancy of a hamster is quite short, possibly the result of its frenetic life cycle. A hamster at the age of two years can be compared to a human of 60. Selective breeding seems to be producing animals that live longer, and hamsters that live beyond three years are now becoming quite common. Quite what age a hamster in the wild would reach is pure conjecture, as predators, food supply, weather conditions and population numbers are all influencing factors.

SPECIES
There are approximately 26 species and subspecies, ranging in size from one of the smallest, Roborovski's Dwarf Russian hamster, to the largest, the European hamster, which is the size of a large guinea pig. Only three of these species are normally kept as pets: the Syrian, the Chinese, and the Dwarfs (including the Campbell, the Winter White and the Roborovski). Chinese hamsters are frequently referred to as part of the Dwarf group, because they share many of the same characteristics, but they are actually a separate species.

2. THE EUROPEAN HAMSTER *(Cricetus cricetus)*
Although the European hamster is not kept as a pet, it is worth mentioning because of its unique qualities among the hamster species. This, the largest variety of hamster, is also known as the Common hamster or the Black Bellied hamster. It has a black chest and underbelly, unlike most other mammals that have lighter-coloured underparts. One of the distinguishing characteristics of the European hamster is its life span – approximately eight years when kept in laboratory conditions – which is far longer than most other species.

Traditionally, farmers have considered the European hamster to be a pest, because it consumed large amounts of crops and significantly damaged the remainder. Today, the European hamster is classed as an endangered species, because pest control has resulted in its incidence in the wild being relatively rare.

European hamsters are rarely kept as pets. They have the reputation of being extremely ferocious, attacking dogs if worried by them and expelling grains from their pouches with such force that serious harm can be inflicted on the target. There have been reports that aggression is reduced when these hamsters are kept in captivity, but as pets they remain extremely rare.

3. THE SYRIAN HAMSTER *(Mesocricetus auratus)*
As the name suggests, the Syrian hamster, originally known as the Golden hamster, originates from Syria. In its natural habitat, this hamster lives in deep burrows, emerging in the cool of night to search for food. The hot, dry, and sometimes arid land means that each hamster has to travel long distances in its search for sustenance and mates. Every Syrian hamster lives a solitary existence once weaned.

DISCOVERY

The first documentary evidence for the Syrian hamster dates from 1797. *The Natural History of Aleppo*, by Alexander Russell (2nd edition), with additional notes by Patrick, his younger brother, records hamsters as present in the Mount Aleppo region of Syria. It is in this second edition, published after the death of Alexander, that we find the first mention of this hamster, so it is possible that it was Patrick who discovered them (although this is pure speculation). There is no mention of the hamster as being a new species, so it must be assumed that they were mistaken for the Common (European) hamster.

An extract from the book illustrates how well the Syrian hamster uses its pouches:

> *"I once found, upon dissecting one of them, the pouch on each side stuffed with young French beans, arranged lengthways so exactly and close to each other, that it appeared strange by what mechanism it had been effected; for the membrane which forms the pouch, though muscular, is thin and the most expert fingers could not have packed the beans in more regular order. When they were laid loosely on the table, they formed a heap three times the bulk of the animal's body."*

CLASSIFICATION

The naming and classification of the Syrian hamster – then known as the Golden hamster – was given by George Waterhouse. In 1839, upon his return from Syria, he presented the skull and skin of a hamster at a meeting of the Zoological Society of London. These remains can still be seen at the Natural History Museum, London, UK. Published in the Society's proceedings for 1840 was Waterhouse's description of the hamster: *"...and is remarkable for its deep golden yellow colouring. The fur is moderately long and very soft and has a silk-like gloss; the deep yellow colouring extends over the upper parts and the sides of the head and body and also over the outer parts of the limbs; on the back the hairs are brownish at the tips, hence this part of the fur assumes a deeper hue than on the sides of the body; the sides of the throat and upper parts of the body are white, but faintly tinted with yellow; on the back and sides of the body, all hairs are of a deep grey or lead colour at the base. The feet and tail are white. The ears are of moderate size, furnished externally with whitish hairs. The moustaches consist of black and white hairs intermixed..."* This could quite easily be a description of one of today's Syrian hamsters.

CAPTIVE SYRIANS

In 1880, a group of hamsters were brought to Edinburgh, Scotland, by British diplomat James Henry Skeene on his retirement. This was most probably the first time that live Syrian hamsters were to be found in the UK, but unfortunately, for reasons unknown, the colony died out after 30 years.

The Syrian hamsters we know and love today are all reported to descend from one mother hamster and her litter. In 1930, Professor Aharoni captured the mother and young from 8 feet (2.4 metres) down a burrow near Mount Aleppo. Reports vary as to how many young were captured, how many escaped, and how many survived to adulthood, but the general consensus is that there were 11 babies and their mother. When the group was placed in a colony box, the mother immediately killed one of the babies. Professor Aharoni, worried that the mother would turn on the rest of the litter, humanely put the mother hamster to sleep. The surviving 10 babies, whose eyes were still closed, then had to be hand-reared. Unfortunately, they escaped and only nine were recaptured. These surviving young were taken back to the Hebrew University in Jerusalem, where five more escaped through the wooden bottom of their cage. The remaining four were bred very successfully, and, in 1931, stock was despatched to various countries, including the UK, to ensure survival of the species should a natural disaster strike the original colony, decimating the numbers. Syrian hamsters made their first arrival in the US in 1938.

THE PET MARKET

By 1937 in the UK, hamsters were making the transition from being kept in laboratories to being kept as pets. By 1945, there were so many people keeping and breeding hamsters that a club was formed. Within a few years, two more clubs were founded, and, in May 1949, the National Hamster Council was inaugurated, which is still in existence today (making it the oldest existing hamster organisation in the world).

In the US, the Syrian hamster gained popularity as a pet throughout the late 1940s and the 1950s. By the middle of the 1980s, hamster enthusiasts had begun forming clubs, although these were 'combined' clubs (i.e. for owners of rats, mice, and other rodents as well as hamsters). Clubs devoted solely to hamsters were not formed until the late 1990s.

Although the hamsters found by Professor Aharoni in 1930 were supposedly the origins of all today's pet hamsters, there are more reports that, as late as 1971, a litter of 12 was found, again in Aleppo. Records show that these 'wild' hamsters became hand-tame and very tractable within three days of handling after arriving in the US, where they again bred successfully. This second litter could account for different mutations appearing in the US and Europe over the years. During 1978, once more in Aleppo, two females were captured and were also taken to the US. A further find, in 1982, resulted in two hamsters being captured, but only one survived, a female, and she was brought to the UK.

PHYSICAL FEATURES

The Syrian hamster grows to between 6 and 8 inches (15 to 20 cms) in length and weighs between 5 and 7 ounces (150 to 200 grams). The general appearance is that of a well-rounded animal with a broad body and head, large erect ears, a Romanesque profile, and large, wide-set eyes. The tail is short, and in the longhaired varieties it is hard to see. A popular description is that it resembles a miniature bear, especially when sitting on its haunches. Indeed, in the US, a longhaired hamster is called a Teddy Bear hamster.

When Syrian hamsters were first kept as pets, only shades (light, normal and dark) of the original golden (mahogany) colour were available. Natural mutations of colour followed in due course, and today there is a wide variety. There have also been coat mutations, namely the satin, the longhaired and the rex, which has further increased the varieties available.

4. THE CHINESE HAMSTER *(Cricetulus griseus)*

Although frequently referred to as a Dwarf hamster, the Chinese hamster is officially classed in the group known as rat-like hamsters. They originate from Mongolia and Northern China, inhabiting the steppes and desert fringes, where the drier conditions are more to their liking.

DISCOVERY AND CLASSIFICATION

The Chinese hamster was first catalogued as early as 1773. Given the name *Cricotulus barabensis* by Pallas in 1773, Milne-Edwards named them *Barabensis griseus* in 1867. Since then, the Chinese hamster has had several other names. In *Systematics of the Mammals of the USSR* (1987), Pavlinov and Rossolimo listed *pseudogriseus* as a separate species, while Corbet and Hill, in *A World List of Mammalian Species* (Third edition, 1991), treated *pseudogriseus* and *griseus* as separate species.

Despite this classification of three different species, other research has shown that the three varieties are actually very similar, at least at chromosomal level. This was thoroughly demonstrated in *Comparison of Karyotypes, G-bands and NORs in Three Cricetulus Species* (1984), by Kral, Radjabli, Graphodatsky and Orlov. Today, most people in the hamster fancy simply use the Latin name *Cricetulus griseus.*

THE PET MARKET

Cricetulus griseus, the Chinese hamster, has been kept in laboratories since 1919 in the UK. Initially, sources suggest that breeding was unsuccessful and that fresh stock had to be captured regularly. However, in the early 1970s, with the successful introduction of the Russian Dwarf hamster to the pet market, interest in the Chinese hamster quickly followed, resulting in more imports and successful attempts at breeding. However, even today, the popularity of the Chinese hamster is not as high as its Russian cousin.

In the US, the Chinese hamster made its first appearance in 1948, when the Harvard Medical School acquired a number of male and female specimens. However, the Chinese hamster has found its popularity hindered by anti-vermin laws, which, in certain states, means that keeping Chinese hamsters as pets is illegal.

PHYSICAL FEATURES

In appearance, Chinese hamsters are the most 'mouse-like' of all the pet hamsters. The body is more slender than broad, measuring approximately 3 inches (8 cms) in length. They have a short tail of about 0.75 inches (2 cms), which exhibits prehensile qualities, while the head is triangular in shape when viewed from above. They are normally a brown-grey colour, with a black stripe down the back and lighter fur on the belly. There has been one natural colour mutation in captivity – the dominant white spot on the body. Very rarely, a white animal with black eyes appears. However, this is not classed as a colour mutation in scientific circles, instead being viewed as a hamster that is all spot and no colour.

One outstanding feature of Chinese hamsters is the ease with which they can be sexed. The male genitalia are extremely prominent, making males easily identifiable. Another feature is that, unlike Syrian hamsters, Chinese hamsters are not always solitary by nature.

5. DWARF RUSSIAN HAMSTERS

There are three varieties of Dwarf Russian hamsters available today. They are the Winter White, the Campbell, and the

Roborovski. Although each variety should be kept separately, more than one individual of that variety can be housed together. Keeping the varieties separate ensures that no crossbreeding can occur, therefore avoiding the creation of any controversial hybrids.

THE WINTER WHITE *(Phodopus sungorus sungorus)*
The Winter White Dwarf Russian hamster comes from Southwest Siberia and Eastern Kazakhstan. Its natural habitat is the grassy steppes, which, in the winter months, have short hours of daylight and low temperatures with persistent snow cover.

DISCOVERY AND CLASSIFICATION
Winter Whites were first catalogued as early as 1773 by Pallas, when they were found in Gratschefskoi, 62 miles (100 kms) west of Semipalatinsk in West Siberia. At that time they were originally classified as belonging to the mouse family, although they were later reclassified as belonging to the hamster family.

THE PET MARKET
Numerous preserved specimens, dating from 1947 onwards, can be found in the Siberian Zoological Museum. However, the pet Winter Whites we know today stem from several animals captured in 1968, in Western Siberia. These hamsters were brought to the Max Planck Institute in Germany, where they were successfully bred in captivity. By the middle of the 1970s, specimens appeared in the Netherlands, with more coming from scientific institutes in Eastern Europe. However, not until the late 1970s did they appear on the UK pet market, and today they are still not as widely available in pet shops as the Campbell.

Winter White hamsters first arrived in America in the early 1980s, although they did not become widespread until a decade later. This was due to anti-vermin laws in some states, which classed hamsters as vermin and prohibited the keeping of hamsters as pets. These laws still apply in some states, while, in other states, keeping hamsters has been made legal only very recently (e.g. California did not permit the keeping of pet hamsters until 1994). The popularity of Winter White hamsters has been slow to grow due to the anti-vermin laws, but they are currently gaining a foothold in America.

PHYSICAL FEATURES
The Winter White has an egg-shaped or oval body, with a broad head. It has prominent black eyes and greyish fur, heavily ticked with black. A black stripe extends down the centre of the back, and along each flank there are three arches of a lighter shade merging into the paler-coloured belly fur. During the winter months in its natural habitat, the Winter White changes colour. Its fur changes to white to match its snow-covered surroundings – hence the popular name of this species – and the characteristic still occurs today if the hamster is kept without artificial light and heat.

Three colour variations have occurred to date – the sapphire (a soft blue-grey), the pearl (white with varying amounts of black ticking), and the sapphire pearl (as the pearl but with the ticking of the sapphire colour). Like the Syrian hamster, the Winter White has a short tail, but compared to the Syrian it is much smaller,

11

growing to about 3 inches (8 cms) only. Occasionally, the Winter White may be referred to as the Western hamster, the Siberian hamster, and (our favourite) the Furry Footed hamster.

THE CAMPBELL *(Phodopus sungorus campbelli)*
The Campbell Dwarf Russian hamster originates from Northern Russia, Northern China and Central Asia. Little is known about the behaviour and natural habitat of this species, but it is normally found on the dry open steppes and sand dunes.

DISCOVERY AND CLASSIFICATION
The Campbell, which may also be known as the Djungarian, the Original and the Western hamster, was first named in 1905. Originally, it was included in the *Phodopus sungorus* family by Corbet in *The Mammals of the Palaearctic Region* (1978), but regarded as a separate species by Pavlinov and Rossolimo in *Systematics of Mammals of the USSR* (1987).

Today, there is still disagreement as to whether the Campbell and the Winter White should be classed as two distinct species or as one. They share many of the same general characteristics, such as the arches, back stripe, thick dense fur, short tail and furry feet. However, the natural colouring of the Campbell is brownish grey – lighter than the Winter White – with a darker black stripe running down the centre of the back and three arches running along each side.

Also, the Campbell is slightly larger than the Winter White, growing to approximately 4 inches (10 cms).

THE PET MARKET
Preserved skins and specimens dating from 1946 can be found in the Siberian Zoological Museum in Novosibirsk, Russia, but the Campbell did not make its appearance in the UK until 1963, with further stock being imported in 1969. By the early 1970s, the Campbell was beginning to appear in UK pet shops, and has become popular ever since. In recent years, many additional colours and coat-types have become available (see page 156).

Campbell hamsters arrived in the US at the same time as their Winter White cousins, and have been subject to the same restrictions. However, as with Winter Whites, recent changes in legislation have seen the popularity of Campbell hamsters greatly increasing, and they are becoming more readily available.

THE ROBOROVSKI *(Phodopus roborovskii)*
The Roborovski Dwarf Russian hamster originates from the sandy desert areas of Northern China and Mongolia. Surprisingly, this little hamster was discovered as far back as 1903, when it was named by Dr K.A. Satunin (Director of the Zoological Museum of the Imperial Academy of St. Petersburg) who found it in Nansham, China.

There is little mention of the species for the next 60 years, and then, in the early 1960s, a colony was established at London Zoo, although it failed to breed.

The present UK stock was imported from Holland in 1990, and can now be found at many UK hamster shows and a limited number of UK pet shops. Although Roborovoskis arrived in the US at the same time as the UK, their availability remains somewhat limited in America.

PHYSICAL FEATURES

'Robos', as they are affectionately called, are the smallest of the pet hamsters, averaging only 1.5 to 2 inches (4 to 5 cms) in length. They have a sandy topcoat, which acts as excellent camouflage from predators, while their pure white belly fur would reflect away the heat from the baking sand. Unlike other Dwarf hamsters they have no dorsal stripe or arches, instead having a white muzzle and large white eyebrows. To date, no colour mutations have occurred. Robos are extremely swift, and, when running on a wheel, their legs appear as a blur.

CHAPTER 2

CHOOSING A HAMSTER

1. Responsibilities
2. Possible problems
3. Hamster appeal
4. Hamster varieties
5. Selective breeding
6. Sexing
7. Health
8. Taking home your hamster

Before making the decision to buy a hamster, consideration must be given to the responsibility of owning a pet that will be dependent on care provided by the owner for the whole of its life. Your pet will need to be fed, watered, handled, loved, and the cage cleaned, none of which should be considered a chore.

1. RESPONSIBILITIES

Hamsters are often described as 'pocket-money pets' because children are able to buy food and bedding out of their pocket money. Purchasing the hamster and its cage is often beyond a child's financial means, but money from birthdays and Christmas, etc., can be put towards the initial cost. For children, saving up for a pet greatly contributes to their having a responsible attitude towards pet ownership. However, even when the hamster is bought and owned by an individual child, the whole family must be involved, because parental guidance is a necessity where the needs of live animals are concerned. Hamsters are not just for children either – they make excellent pets for people of all ages.

Caring for a hamster is not particularly burdensome. Hamster cages, although varied in design, materials, and size, can be kept in almost any part of the house, the exception being conservatories or other, similar rooms with excessive heat or direct sunlight.

By nature, the hamster is a very clean creature, designating areas of its cage to store its food, to make its nest, and to use as a toilet area. Provided that the cage is thoroughly cleaned once a week, there is little or no smell from a hamster cage. This means that even the largest of cages can be accommodated in most homes.

Daily feeding and water checks are essential, as are exercise periods. Unlike many pets, hamsters do not require regular outdoor exercise, which makes them easy pets to care for. As long as the cage is well situated (see page 28), and the hamster is handled regularly and given plenty of opportunity for exercising outside its cage under its owner's supervision (see page 45), this is normally sufficient.

2. POSSIBLE PROBLEMS

Hamsters have a reputation for biting, which we feel is a defamation of character. Biting is often the result when someone pokes a finger through the bars of the cage and the hamster, because of its poor eyesight, assumes it is food. It is possible that a finger poked through the bars may also be taken as an invasion of the hamster's territory and it reacts accordingly. A finger poked into the nest of a sleeping hamster nearly always results in a bite because the hamster is frightened. Handled correctly, hamsters very rarely bite.

The average life span of a pet hamster is approximately two years, which is a point that should be considered before buying your pet. The short life span may pose emotional problems for younger children, and, in some cases, adults who become very attached to their pet. That said, although two years is the norm, many hamsters are now living beyond this age.

3. HAMSTER APPEAL

While every pet requires time and responsibility from its owner, the rewards far outweigh the demands for the hamster owner. Hamsters can be great fun to keep, and quite a strong bond can be established between hamster and owner.

CURIOSITY

One advantage of keeping a pet that lives in a cage is the hours of entertainment that can be derived simply from watching the hamster go about its daily routine. Hamsters are naturally curious. This is exhibited from an early age – everything has to be tasted, smelled and explored. Adults love exploring new territory, feeling and tasting lots of things on their wanderings.

Hamsters have excellent hearing, and, while awake, their ears are held erect to catch sound. Hamsters respond well to the human voice, and, if talked to from an early age, will learn to come when called. Many of ours appear to know their names and will come to the cage door when their name is called. Most will surface from sleep to become aware of a human presence, but will wait to see if the visit concerns them before leaving the nest. The more inquisitive cannot resist coming out to find out what, if anything, is happening – whatever the time of day. Many people assume that as the hamster is naturally nocturnal it should not be disturbed during the day. However, we have found that this is not at all the case.

ENDEARING EYES

Part of a hamster's appeal is its large eyes, but, as with many nocturnal animals, eyesight is poor. Hamsters appear to notice movements from above, but it is debatable whether these movements are seen by the eyes or 'seen' by a combination of other senses. Movements from above may result in the hamster turning onto its back in a defensive position. For example, a young hamster will often do this when a hand descends on it unexpectedly from above. Frequently, this defensive posture is accompanied by squeaking sounds of fright, which can be very alarming to the owner.

VERSATILE FEET

One of the hamster's most endearing characteristics is the way in which it uses its front paws or feet to hold its food and to groom. A hamster's paws are extremely dexterous, and in certain situations (e.g. when stripping off the outer husk from a sunflower seed) they bear a resemblance to human hands. The speed with which pouches are filled and emptied using the front feet is quite unbelievable.

CHEEK POUCHES

The whole facial appearance of a hamster changes when it fills its cheek pouches. These pouches, which run from chin to under ear, have a special lining and are extremely elastic, to allow for accommodation of vast quantities of food or bedding. When full, the pouches betray the outline of the foods stored in them, and the hamster appears to have a bad case of mumps! Gorgeous, a large Syrian female of ours, once pouched 146 sunflower seeds! (These were surreptitiously removed from her nest at a later time, as too many sunflower seeds are not good for hamsters.) When the hamster wants to empty its pouches, it uses its front paws, pushing on the external side of the pouches to push the contents back inside the mouth.

4. HAMSTER VARIETIES

Before purchasing a hamster, the potential owner should thoroughly research the different varieties, with their different requirements.

SYRIAN

Syrian hamsters are normally more widely available in pet shops than other varieties. Furthermore, because of the coat and colour variations, there is a huge selection from which to choose.

The Syrian hamster is the largest of the pet hamster varieties, and therefore, from the point of view of size, might be considered slightly easier to handle. However, remember that, in general, a Syrian will need larger accommodation than the smaller varieties. The golden rule for this variety is one hamster, one cage. Syrian hamsters are solitary by nature, and by the age of six or seven weeks (sometimes even earlier), they show definite tendencies to want their own territories. Never make the mistake, when viewing a group of young hamsters cuddled together in the nest, of buying two because "one on its own might be lonely". Be assured that, within a couple of days, one or other of them will claim the cage or tank as its own territory and fighting will ensue. The results of this fighting can be very serious, leading to injury or even death.

MALE OR FEMALE?

Unusually, females tend be bigger than males. Both males and females show the same inquisitiveness and curiosity, but the male is generally the more placid. We have found that females can exhibit far more personality. For the first-time owner, a male is generally more suitable, but, as each hamster is an individual with its own personality and temperament, a decision may need to be left until you view your prospective pet.

LONG OR SHORTHAIRED?

Shorthaired hamsters require little or no grooming from their owners, and can be kept on sawdust, woodchips, or shavings. Of the longhaired Syrians, only the male grows long hair; the female develops a fluffy coat rather than a longhaired one. This means that there is minimal grooming required for the female, but the male needs more attention. It is easier to keep very longhaired males on sawdust, as woodchips or shavings encourage tangling if caught in the hair.

Shorthaired hamsters are the better choice for anyone suffering from asthma or another allergy. However, before buying a hamster, asthma sufferers would do best to borrow a friend's hamster for a few days, to make sure they do not suffer any adverse reactions. Asthma sufferers should use wood shavings as a bedding material, as this is less likely to cause an attack.

As well as different hair lengths, there are three types of coat available – the normal coat, the satin coat (soft and shiny), and the rex coat (curly whiskers and slightly curly hair).

WHAT COLOUR?

This is purely a matter of personal preference, and there is no shortage of colours from which to choose. As well as different colours, Syrian hamsters come in a variety of patterned coats, including bands (a circle of white around the body), spots (a hamster with white spots), and roans (white, heavily ticked with colour). More information on colours can be found in chapter 10.

SUMMARY
- Only one per cage
- Suitable for all ages, but parental guidance is a necessity for children under eight
- Large variety of choice
- More readily available than other varieties.

CHINESE

Chinese hamsters can be very shy, often choosing to hide underneath their bedding and shavings. They love tunnelling and are excellent climbers, appreciating small branches and ropes to play with. This makes them very entertaining to watch and so more suitable for the older child or adult.

Chinese hamsters can be kept singly, in pairs (either single sex or mixed), or in colonies. However, it should be noted that squabbles can occur between mature animals and it may be necessary to separate them if fighting escalates. Also remember, if keeping mixed-sex groups, that nature may eventually take its course and a population explosion is only to be expected.

MALE OR FEMALE?

As far as temperament is concerned, there is no real difference between the sexes. If keeping a single sex group, it is perhaps better to opt for males as they seem more tolerant of each other's company. However, we have kept pairs of females together without too much discord, so again, personal preference would be the determining factor.

Another point to remember is that the genitals of the male are very much in evidence, and some people may find this somewhat obtrusive.

WHAT COLOUR?

Currently, there are only two colours available – the normal and the dominant spot. The dominant spot can have varying amounts of white, ranging from very little to an almost totally white animal that could, theoretically, be classed as a separate colour. There is no difference in temperament between the colours, so any decision is down to personal preference.

SUMMARY

- More than one may be kept together
- More suitable for older children and adults
- Limited choice of colours
- Not as readily available in pet shops as the Syrian hamster.

CAMPBELL

This variety is more curious and outgoing than the Chinese, spending a lot of time exercising and exploring. Campbells may be a little quick for very young children and may also nip if held for too long. However, a good-natured Campbell is a joy to have as a pet, and, having judged many pet hamster shows, we can say that a Campbell has quite often run away with first prize.

In the UK, diabetes is known to exist in some lines, so care must be taken to select healthy stock. Therefore, make sure you acquire your hamster from a reputable source and that you ask whether the hamster you are buying has any history of diabetes in its parentage. We are not aware of any reported cases of diabetes among hamsters in the US.

As with the Chinese, Campbell hamsters can be kept singly, in pairs (either single-sex or mixed), or in colonies, and the same problems can occur with squabbling in mature animals, which may require the hamsters to be separated. Campbells seem to be very vocal, and although fights may sound serious, this may not be the case. It is well worth examining individuals for bites (usually on the tummy) before considering separation. If contemplating a mixed-sex group or pair, it is advisable to remember that litters can be expected approximately every 18 days once the pair or group starts breeding.

MALE OR FEMALE?

There is no real difference in temperament between the two sexes. However, many keepers consider males to be easier to keep together. This is because most females in any given group will each try to establish themselves as matriarch of the colony, which can lead to significant levels of squabbling.

WHAT COLOUR?

As with the Syrian hamster, there are now many colour variations available, although some of the newer ones are available from specialist breeders only. As well as the normal (original) colour, mutations have occurred that include albino (white with red eyes), argenté (sandy-coloured), mottled (spotted), black, platinum black, and dove. A full list of colours can be found in chapter 10.

In addition to the standard coat type, two mutations have appeared: the satin (with a sheen that makes the hamster look slightly damp) and the rex (with its slightly curly, but at present very sparse, coat).

SUMMARY
- More than one may be kept together
- More suitable for older children and adults
- Many colours available, but not all can be found in pet shops
- Diabetes present in some lines.

WINTER WHITE
The Winter White shares many characteristics with the Campbell, being fairly outgoing, fond of exercising (particularly on wheels), prone to vocalising, and liable to squabble with other hamsters. However, the Winter White tends to have a more equable temperament when being handled, although they are not the ideal choice for younger children. Winter Whites reproduce at slightly longer intervals than Campbells (a day or two longer), but anyone keeping mixed-sex groups would do well to remember that this can still result in an awful lot of baby hamsters in a very short time!

MALE OR FEMALE?
There is no difference in temperament between males and females, but if you intend to keep a single-sex group, males would be the best choice as females have a stronger tendency to fight.

WHAT COLOUR?
At present, only four colours are readily available: the 'normal' (grey), the sapphire (grey with a blue tinge, with the dorsal stripe), the normal pearl and the sapphire pearl (both pearls are white animals with varying degrees of black ticking).

SUMMARY
- More than one may be kept together
- More suitable for older children and adults
- Not as readily available in pet shops as the Campbell
- Limited choice of colours available.

ROBOROVSKI
When it comes to entertainment value, the Roborovski is unequalled. Robos tend to spend more daylight time awake than all the other species, running on their wheel, exploring their cages, and generally being busy. Although they are very unlikely to bite, their supersonic speed makes them unsuitable as a child's pet – it is far too easy for this hamster to be dropped or to jump.

Robos can be kept singly or in single- or mixed-sex groups. In our experience, a single Robo seems to be quite happy as long as it has a wheel to run on and a variety of things to play with.

Roborovski hamsters are not yet abundant in pet shops, but their availability is increasing all the time. If you are interested in keeping this variety, you should be able to purchase them from a specialist breeder or at a hamster show.

MALE OR FEMALE?
From information available to us at this time, the sex of the hamster seems to make no difference except to another hamster!

WHAT COLOUR?
The choice is limited to one, the original colour. No colour mutations have appeared to date.

SUMMARY
• More than one may be kept together
• More suitable for teenagers and adults
• No choice of colour
• Not readily available in pet shops.

5. HAMSTER SOURCES

As with all pets, it is best to purchase direct from a breeder that has been recommended to you, either by a friend or by a hamster organisation. Failing this, a hamster show is another option. Shows are likely to have a varied selection of species and colours, and all the stock should come from recognised exhibitors. Purchasing from a reputable breeder, either privately or at a show, carries the added advantage that you can talk to the breeder about diet and care, and the hamster will be accompanied by a 'birth certificate'. The certificate will display a contact address or telephone number, so the breeder can be contacted at a future time should you have any queries.

If you cannot find a breeder or a show local to you, and you decide to purchase a hamster from a pet shop, make sure you choose one that has a good reputation – personal recommendation is best. Although you will always hear horrific stories concerning pet shops and their stock, generally, these are in the minority. Some of our stock has come from pet shops, because we cannot resist entering one and nosing through the cages. One such purchase started a bloodline, which produced many Best In Shows.

6. SEXING

If you purchase your hamster from a reputable pet shop, breeder, or at a show, ask the vendor to show you how to tell the sexes apart. They should be able to show you very quickly and easily. However, if the vendor is unsure, or if your hamster has come from a friend, you may need to check for yourself, once you become accustomed to handling your pet.

Hold the hamster so that its back is against the palm of your hand, your thumb is under its chin, and its rear end is by your little finger. Make sure you hold your hand so that the hamster's head is uppermost and its rear end is hanging over the edge of your hand slightly. In this position, the hamster's genitals should be clearly

Male and Female

Male

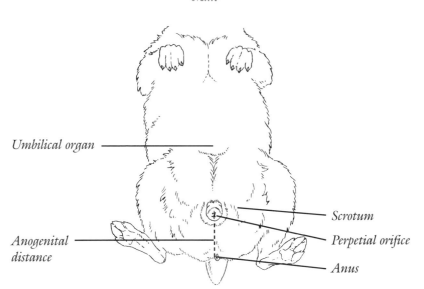

Umbilical organ

Anogenital distance

Scrotum

Perpetial orifice

Anus

Female

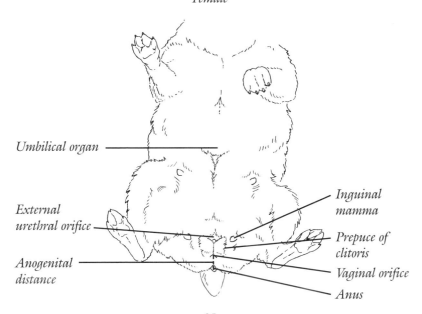

Umbilical organ

External urethral orifice

Anogenital distance

Inguinal mamma

Prepuce of clitoris

Vaginal orifice

Anus

21

exposed. In females, the openings will be very close together in a 'bald' patch, whereas in males there is a gap, with fur between the two openings.

SYRIAN
The sex of Syrian hamsters, especially the shorthaired variety, can be distinguished by the shape of the rear end. Females have a rounded rear, while the male has a more pointed rear, which usually protrudes slightly.

Syrians should be in single-sex groups by five weeks of age. Beyond this, they are sexually mature and any female from a mixed group could be pregnant. We have had many calls from people who have purchased a hamster and several days later had some unexpected additions to the family. We started with a single female Syrian hamster and six days later we had seven (mum and six babies)!

ROBOROVSKI
As with Syrian hamsters, Roborovski hamsters should be in single-sex groups by the age of five weeks. Although Robos normally mature later, they may be sexually active by this age, and it is better to be safe than sorry.

Robos can be more difficult to sex than other hamsters because of their small size. However, an experienced breeder, keeper, or vet will be able to tell the difference. If the vendor tells you that the babies are too young to sex, or that they can only be sexed by a vet, this is more than likely to be an excuse to cover up the fact that the vendor is not experienced enough to sex the babies.

CHINESE/OTHER DWARF SPECIES
As with Syrian hamsters, Dwarf and Chinese hamsters should be in single-sex groups by the age of five weeks. Chinese hamsters, and most Dwarf species, normally mature later than five weeks, but there are always exceptions.

If you intend to keep a single-sex pair of hamsters, ask the vendor to double-check the sex of the animals you have chosen. Ensure that the two you have chosen have genital areas that look the same, so that, even if you end up with the wrong sex (e.g. two males as opposed to two females), you do not have the possibility of having an unwanted litter in a few months time. Choose two animals of roughly the same size – one will nearly always be dominant over the other, but if both are the same size, the subservient one will be better able to withstand any attempts at bullying.

7. HEALTH
Whatever variety of hamster you decide to buy, a few simple guidelines are applicable:
- Baby hamsters for sale should be a minimum of four weeks old and completely weaned. Always ask the age of the babies before buying.
- Check the hamster's eyes, which should be bright and alert.
- Check the hamster for fresh bites or wounds. Never buy a hamster with open wounds. Minor nicks in the ears, however, may have occurred when the hamster was very young. If the wounds have healed, the injuries can be ignored.
- Look for a high standard of cleanliness in the cages containing the hamsters. Is there enough food and water? An empty water bottle may mean the hamsters have been without water for some time, and they may be dehydrated.

- The runt of a hamster litter is normally quite healthy, and will join in with its littermates in play and feeding. However, while the smallest may look the sweetest, unless you know its background you would do better to choose a more robust hamster.
- Any hamster that sits quietly in a corner, or stays in the nest showing no interest in food or what is going on, should be avoided. It is quite likely that the hamster is sickening for something or is already unwell.
- Ask for the hamster of your choice to be brought out for a closer examination. Watch to see how it is handled and how the hamster reacts to handling. You should be able to gauge whether the hamster is used to being handled, allowing for the fact that young hamsters may be bouncy and nervous. If the vendor uses gloves to handle the hamster, or if the hamster is ushered into a box to be shown to you without being handled at all, consider buying your hamster from another outlet.
- Ask the vendor if you can buy a few days' supply of the hamster's food. Sudden changes in diet can upset a hamster's tummy, so it is best to stick to the hamster's established diet for a few days. Remember that any dietary changes you introduce after that should be very gradual and in small quantities.

8. TAKING HOME YOUR HAMSTER

Once you've decided on the hamster or hamsters you want, you need to make sure that you can get them home safely. Ideally, your decision to keep a hamster will have been made well in advance of your buying one, in order to give yourself time to choose the right species, to buy the equipment, and to make the necessary preparations at home. If you have followed this path, you should have bought a small, plastic travelling container, for transporting your hamster to the vet, etc. This is ideal for transporting your hamster from the breeder or pet shop.

If you do not have a carry case, a responsible vendor will offer you one. However, remember that the cardboard boxes offered by some vendors offer little or no protection against the gnawing of a hamster's teeth, and your hamster may have chewed its way out before you arrive home. If your hamster escapes, even inside a car, it may be extremely awkward to catch – if indeed you can. An effective, inexpensive alternative to cardboard boxes or a special travelling case is a clean, plastic 7-pint (4-litre) container (e.g. an ice cream container), with air holes punched in the lid.

Once you get your hamster home, you should put it inside its new cage immediately, with plenty of fresh food and water. Leave the hamster alone for the rest of the day, so that it has time to become accustomed to its new home and can settle in without any disturbances.

CHAPTER 3

HOUSING YOUR HAMSTER

1. Wire-top cages
2. Plastic-tank cages
3. Glass-tank cages
4. Laboratory cages
5. Homemade cages
6. Choosing the right cage
7. Setting up home

The type of home you choose for your prospective new pet will be dependent on what species of hamster you have chosen, how many hamsters you have, where in the house you want to keep the cage, and some other considerations, such as pets, etc. There is a huge choice of cage types and sizes, and it would be impossible for us to give an opinion on every one. Each of the different types available is described in general terms here, together with an opinion on their suitability for the different hamster species.

1. WIRE-TOP CAGES

This type of cage is perhaps the most varied of all the cages, available in single, double and triple storeys, with ladders or tubes connecting the levels. It consists of a plastic tray base, with a rigid wire top. The floors in the multi-storey cages are made of wire or solid plastic.

Wire-top cages tend to come in two bar-width varieties (i.e. the space between the bars of the cage). Some cages have a gap of approximately 0.5 inches (12 mm) between the cage bars, which is suitable for Syrians only, while other cages have a bar gap of 0.3 inches (8 mm), suitable for Chinese and Dwarf hamsters as well as Syrian hamsters.

It should be noted that the cages with the narrower 0.3 inches (8 mm) gap normally come in smaller sizes. These smaller cages may be advertised as mouse

24

cages rather than hamster cages, and they may not be big enough to house a Syrian hamster. Also remember that the total floor area may be the same in a single-storey cage as it is in a multi-storey cage, particularly if the multi-storey model only has partial floors. If you decide to buy a multi storey cage, make sure there is access to each level so that you can pick up your pet from any part of the cage. Multi-storey cages with only one door can make picking up your hamster very difficult.

DESIGN FAULTS
Some wire-top cages have design faults that make them unsuitable. Avoid cages that have ladders positioned over the doorway, too few doors (one door per level is best), wrongly hinged doors (i.e. doors that open upwards instead of downwards or sideways), and unstable levels (a rocking floor may make a hamster nervous). In multi-storey cages ensure that the hamster cannot fall directly from roof to cage floor. Ideally, access to each floor level should be on alternate sides of the cage.

Before you buy this type of cage, check the catches that secure the wire top to the plastic base. If these are not secure, the base may become separated from the rest of the cage when you lift it up. Not only will this make a mess if the cage is already made up, but it could also result in your hamster escaping or sustaining an injury.

2. PLASTIC-TANK CAGES
Plastic-tank cages come in all sorts of shapes and sizes, depending on the manufacturer. Some are little more than plastic aquarium-type containers, while others may be highly elaborate, consisting of multiple modules/tanks, connected by tunnels. Most of these sorts of cages can be expanded as and when the owner chooses.

When you purchase your first unit, please consider the fact that many of the so-called 'starter' packs are not, in our opinion, big enough to house a Syrian hamster. Also remember that not everything included in the pack may be used by your hamster and could take up valuable floor space unnecessarily. Dwarfs and Chinese hamsters sometimes find it difficult to climb the interconnecting tubes unaided, especially when young. However, you can overcome this problem by buying small ladders or climbing aids to insert in the vertical tubes. Alternatively, you can expand the unit horizontally.

Another type of plastic tank looks like a large plant propagator with a large wire door in the top to allow for a two-handed pick-up. These come in various sizes and with a variety of fixtures and fittings. Also available are cages that combine elements of the plastic-tank cage and the wire-top cage. They consist of a plastic-tank base with a second level made out of wire. The plastic-tank base protects the hamster from draughts and allows for plenty of burrowing opportunities, while the wire top can be used for climbing. Another advantage of this cage is that the wire top can be removed to allow easy access to your hamster. As with all wire cages, remember that the space between the wires will determine which species can be kept.

PROBLEMS
Hamsters love gnawing things, and they need to gnaw in order to keep their teeth in good condition. One of the problems with plastic-tank cages is that hamsters – particularly Syrians – can gnaw them to destruction in a very short time. This can be avoided by making sure that you supply your hamster with plenty of gnawing

material. You should also examine the cage closely at regular intervals, looking for any areas that a hamster has already gnawed, so facilitating escape.

One of the problems with plastic-tank module cages is that they can make it very difficult to retrieve your hamster. Nervous hamsters will head straight for a tunnel and disappear to another module if a hand suddenly appears where they are. However, once you have accustomed your hamster to coming to the cage door when called, this should not be a problem. The newer versions of this cage type incorporate larger doors, which make access to your hamster easier.

POSITIONING

If you decide to buy any type of plastic-tank cage, care should be taken when you position the tank at home. Heat and condensation can build up very quickly in a plastic cage. However, the plastic offers protection for the hamster against draughts, and also has the added advantage that shavings are confined to the cage, as opposed to all over the floor (as normally happens with wire cages). Furthermore, younger members of the family, who cannot resist poking their fingers through the bars of wire cages, are less likely to get bitten if the hamster is in a plastic tank.

3. GLASS-TANK CAGES

Glass-tank cages include converted aquariums and purpose-designed glass tanks for small animals. Both are equally suitable for all varieties of hamster, depending on size.

Purpose-designed tanks have come onto the market only recently. They come in a variety of sizes, making them suitable for all species of hamster. Depending on the size of the tank, there will be a number of internal floor levels, and some tanks will have special features, such as shelves, ventilation, and special covers. Obviously, your hamster cannot chew glass, so make sure you provide plenty of gnawing material for your hamster, so that it can wear down its teeth without damaging itself or any of the plastic components of the cage.

As with plastic tanks, care needs to be taken when positioning a glass tank. Remember too, that a glass tank is very heavy, and you will need to be able to gain easy access to clean it. Although heavy to handle when cleaning, the weight of a glass tank can be a distinct advantage in a household with inquisitive children or curious pets.

CONVERTED AQUARIUMS

Many people use converted aquariums to house hamsters, and a modified aquarium can make a great hamster home. Firstly, the standard aquarium cover will need to be replaced with something more suitable for hamsters. The normal cover is not suitable because it encourages condensation and is relatively easy for a hamster to remove. An easy way to make a cover is to use 0.5-inch-square (or 1-cm-square) wire mesh, cut so that just over an inch (3 cms) extends beyond the glass edge. This overlap should be bent down and a piece of elastic attached to each corner. Stick four self-adhesive cup hooks, upside down, to the outside of the tank, towards the bottom of each corner. The elastic on the corners of the wire mesh can then be looped under the cup hooks, making a secure, well-ventilated cover to the aquarium. Water bottles, designed to hang in tanks, are easily available, as are freestanding wheels, so you can kit out your hamster's cage in any way you like.

4. LABORATORY CAGES

As the name suggests, these cages are normally used in laboratories, and are designed for ease of feeding and cleaning. They consist of a relatively deep, hard plastic tray, on to which clips a flat wire grid. The grid usually has two depressions, one to accommodate a water bottle and the other to hold a handful of food pellets. They can be used to house all hamster varieties depending on the size of the cage and the gaps between the cage bars – only the largest are suitable for Syrian hamsters.

Laboratory cages are not aesthetically pleasing, but they enable fanciers to keep a larger number of hamsters because of the ease with which they can be cleaned. Furthermore, feeding and checking can be done without needing to open the cage, making routine care quick and easy without the risk of losing the hamster. However, be wary of buying a laboratory cage for the wrong reasons. They are not a cheaper option. Indeed, laboratory cages can cost double, or even triple, the amount paid for an equivalent commercial cage.

5. HOMEMADE CAGES

WOODEN CAGES

Over the years we have been asked many times for our opinion on homemade wooden cages. If designed and built with a gnawing rodent in mind, they can make excellent homes, but a number of important considerations must be borne in mind.

Wooden cages must always be made out of untreated wood. Paint and varnish can be highly toxic to small animals. For similar reasons, plywood or composition wood should not be used as both contain glue, which may be ingested by a gnawing hamster. Another thing to remember is that wooden cages will absorb urine, and, therefore, they will need to be cleaned more thoroughly and allowed to dry for longer than any of the cages mentioned above. You may also need to make ongoing repairs.

Despite the work involved in them, wooden cages can make ideal homes. When our hamsters decided to reproduce, we made our own wooden cages, using a standard rabbit hutch. We replaced the wire on the door with 0.5-inch-square (or 1-cm-square) wire mesh, and covered any exposed struts with the same material. If you are thinking of housing Dwarf or Chinese hamsters, remember to use wire mesh with a smaller gauge.

At one point, we had 72 wooden cages in our hamstery. However, we found that the work involved in cleaning this number of cages (including ongoing repairs) was excessive. Eventually, we replaced all the wooden cages with commercial ones, which cut our cleaning time in half – a point to remember if you do not have the time to clean wooden cages as thoroughly and as often as necessary.

TEMPORARY HOMEMADE CAGES

Occasionally, you may need another cage or two, but you may be unable to purchase one at the time, or unwilling to buy one because you will only need it for a short time. You can make some great temporary cages, either using a square, plastic washing-up bowl, or a plastic storage box.

If you use a washing-up bowl, 0.5-inch-square (or 1-cm-square) wire mesh can be used to cover the top with a small overlap bent under the top lip. If one end is left unbent, it is possible to slide off the mesh for ease of access. A standard water bottle can be used to provide water by placing the nozzle through the mesh.

You can make a lid for a storage box in the same way as described for glass tanks (see page 26). You may need a hanging-style water bottle if the box is fairly deep.

Temporary cages like these are suitable for all varieties of hamster, provided that they are not kept in them for too long. They are also very handy if you have squabbling hamsters that need separating for a few days, prior to re-homing.

6. CHOOSING THE RIGHT CAGE

Whatever type of cage you decide to buy, make sure you buy the biggest you can reasonably afford. Remember that the most expensive is not necessarily the best. Although a cage may look pretty, it is not always practical – try to look at the cage from your hamster's point of view.

7. SETTING UP HOME

Ideally, you should have bought a cage, and made it ready for your hamster, before you buy your pet. This will prevent your hamster from becoming stressed in its travelling container while it waits for its future home to be set up.

As well as the cage, you will need shavings, bedding material, a food bowl, a water bottle, and a supply of food. Some or all of these may be included with the cage you have bought.

POSITIONING THE CAGE

Think carefully about where you are going to position your hamster's cage. It must be out of direct sunlight, away from any draughts, and not too near any sources of direct heat, such as radiators.

Place the cage on a stable surface, in a position where it cannot be accidentally knocked to the floor. A room with a constant temperature (even if on the cooler side) is better than a room with large temperature fluctuations. Ensure that the cage, especially if you have a wire-top one, is not placed close to soft furnishings, such as curtains or armchairs – your hamster will not be able to resist adding some of this material to its bedding.

If you have bought a wire-top cage, you may be concerned about the amount of bedding material your hamster will throw out through the bars. You can overcome this problem by making a simple 'tidy box'. You will need a cardboard box, approximately 4 inches (10 cms) bigger than the base of the cage. Cut down the box so that it is approximately 2 inches (5 cms) higher than the top of the plastic tray, and then place the cage in the tidy box. The box should catch most of the discarded shavings. You can decorate the box to match the décor of the room or cage.

SHAVINGS

Whether you buy shavings, woodchips or sawdust will depend on the type of hamster you intend to buy. For example, sawdust is normally the best option for a longhaired Syrian hamster. However, very fine sawdust has been known to irritate a hamster's eyes and nose, so is best avoided. Standard wood shavings are the most readily available floor covering and the preferred choice of most breeders.

Whatever floor covering you decide on, make sure that it is intended for use by small animals. It is advisable not to purchase your shavings from builders' merchants or sawmills, as they could contain wood preservatives. Commercially packaged shavings, packaged especially for small animals, will be free from this type of contamination.

Concern has been voiced about the oil content of cedar shavings, which can cause irritation, so these should be avoided. Never use newspaper as a floor covering, even if it is placed underneath a layer of shavings. Newsprint can contain substances that may be harmful to your hamster if it decides to shred the newspaper for extra bedding material.

Once you have bought your floor covering, you will need to spread a layer, approximately 0.7 inches (2 cms) deep, all over the base of the cage. This layer will absorb the hamster's urine and keep the cage smelling sweet. Your hamster may also mix it with its bedding material to enlarge its nest.

BEDDING MATERIAL
With the exception of hamster wheels, this is the most controversial subject when it comes to setting up your hamster's home.

COTTON WOOL (COTTON)
Some years ago, the fluffy, cotton wool (cotton) type of bedding was introduced to the pet market. Since then, there have been many scares as to the safety of this product. The problem stems from the fact that the synthetic version cannot be easily digested if swallowed and may cause intestinal blockages.

If you decide to buy this type of bedding, please ensure that the packet is marked 'made from natural plant fibres' or 'made from reconstituted cellulose', which indicates that it should be digestible. Some packets are marked 'If you see your hamster eating this, please remove immediately', and these should be avoided.

Unfortunately, once this type of bedding is removed from the packet it is impossible for anyone (except perhaps a scientist) to tell one type from another. If you are at all unsure about whether the bedding is made from natural fibres or is synthetically produced, do not use it. However, that said, we have known many owners who, over the years, have kept their hamsters on this type of bedding with no problems.

HAY
An alternative bedding material is hay. This works particularly well for Syrian hamsters, although if you have a longhaired Syrian, you might do best to avoid hay as it can tangle in the long fur. As with any product used in your hamster's cage, make sure any hay you use is intended for use by small animals. Hay collected from fields or untreated bales may contain mites, which will cause your hamster problems. Never use straw, which, due to its sharp ends, can cause injury to the hamster's cheek pouches and eyes.

Many breeders keeping Dwarf or Chinese hamsters choose to use shavings only, as the hamsters love to burrow in them, piling up the shavings to make a nest. However, in our experience, an addition of some paper bedding is not unwelcome.

SHREDDED PAPER

By far the most popular choice of bedding among breeders is shredded paper, which is normally one of the cheapest as well. Do not be tempted to use shredded paper from an office because the print on the paper may be toxic and there may be wire staples mixed in with it. Commercial paper bedding is easily and cheaply available, and comes in many forms – plain or coloured, and in long strands or confetti-like pieces.

A plus for using plain white paper bedding is that any problems with health (loose droppings, slight blood loss, etc.) are immediately evident, and, should you keep white or light-coloured animals, there is no danger of staining should the bedding get damp. Green Peace, a rescued hamster of ours, had been kept in a modular cage. Her green-coloured bedding had become damp, and because she was a white hamster, her fur had been stained an unbecoming shade of green that took two or three months to moult out. If keeping longhaired male Syrian hamsters, we would suggest the use of the long-stranded paper bedding, which will help keep tangles to a minimum.

HOW MUCH?

How much bedding you give your hamster will, of course, depend on the species and the type of bedding you choose. If you give too much you may find that, by the time the hamster has fluffed it up, it has filled the whole cage. The amount of bedding required will also depend on the season; more will be required during the colder months.

If you own a multi-storey cage, put the bedding on the bottom level initially. Once your hamster has decided where it will sleep and moved the bedding, it can be replaced in that spot when you clean the cage.

WATER BOTTLES

Although dishes can be used for water, in our experience these quickly become soiled with shavings and need to be checked at least twice a day. Water bottles are by far the easiest and cleanest way to provide water. There are water bottles to suit all styles of cage, including those designed specifically for use in aquariums or tanks.

The water bottle should be placed in the cage at the right height for the hamster, so that it does not have to stretch too far to reach the spout. The water level should be checked daily, and fresh water should be provided regularly. Different hamsters will drink different amounts, but, if fresh greens are provided, the amount of water drunk will normally decrease.

FOOD DISHES

Today, many cages come complete with food dishes, either included in the package, or incorporated into the design of the cage. If your cage does not come with food dishes, you can choose between dishes made of plastic, ceramics, or stainless steel. An inexpensive alternative is the plastic lid from a coffee jar, with the cardboard insert removed. A food dish is not a necessity – the hamster will normally empty it and put the food in its store – but we humans do not seem to like the idea of putting the food directly onto wood shavings, so we insist on a food dish of some kind.

Once the cage is set up with shavings, bedding and water, put some food in the food dish and place it on the bottom level of the cage.

ACCESSORIES

Some of the following accessories may come included with your cage, while others will need to be purchased separately. You should be able to purchase any of these accessories from a good pet shop.

HAMSTER WHEELS

Most cages come with a wheel included, although some are more practical than others. Many cage designers have not appreciated that hamsters, especially Syrians, now grow much larger than their counterparts of the past. Consequently, a wheel that is suitable for your young hamster will not necessarily accommodate it when it is fully grown. When your hamster grows, you can replace the original wheel with a large, solid plastic one.

It is always preferable to have a solid plastic wheel, as opposed to the wire or slotted-plastic wheel, where there is a danger of limbs becoming trapped. If your cage comes with an open-rung wheel, you can either cover the outside of the wheel with a strip of cardboard, or you can weave a piece of cardboard through the rungs. This will prevent the hamster's limbs from falling through the gaps. You will, of course, need to replace the cardboard frequently, as and when it becomes chewed.

If your cage is glass or plastic, self-standing and hanging wheels are available. With a little ingenuity you can adapt ordinary clip-on wheels to hang in a tank, using a length of bent wire.

If you keep Dwarf or Chinese hamsters, you may like to try an alternative type of wheel, which resembles a TV satellite dish. If you have more than one hamster, it is a good idea to have more than one wheel, as this may alleviate squabbling.

HAMSTER HOUSES

If your cage comes complete with a house, do not put it in the cage for the first few weeks as it may hinder the taming and handling of your new pet. If, after this time, you want to provide your hamster with a house, make sure it has adequate ventilation holes. A build-up of condensation could lead to damp bedding, which can, in turn, cause health problems.

HAMSTER TOILETS

Hamsters, by nature, are very clean and normally designate an area of their cage as a 'wet corner'. Some manufactures have been quick to seize on this, and have designed 'hamster toilets'. Unfortunately, some of these are a little small for today's Syrian hamsters. A large jar laid on its side serves the same purpose.

As with a hamster house, the hamster toilet should not be put in the cage while your hamster is settling in. Give your hamster a few weeks to settle in before introducing the toilet or jar. The hamster can be encouraged to use the toilet by putting a small amount of soiled shavings from the 'wet corner' into the toilet and placing the toilet back in the 'wet corner'. This may need to be done for several days before the hamster will use it as a toilet. The toilet can then be cleaned as often as necessary. However, do not be disappointed or surprised if your hamster refuses to use its 'toilet', deciding instead to use it as a store for its food.

SAND BATHS

A fairly large, food-type dish, half filled with chinchilla sand, makes an excellent 'sand bath' for Dwarf hamsters. You will find they love rolling upside down in the fine sand.

OTHER ACCESSORIES

You need only walk into a pet shop to see just how many hamster toys and accessories are available. However, always remember that they are accessories, not necessities. Also remember that a cage overcrowded with toys can be just as claustrophobic for your hamster as a small cage devoid of toys. If you would like to provide your hamster with toys, but feel that the cage is not big enough to accommodate them, you could create a hamster 'play box' or 'activity playground' (see page 46).

Before buying any accessories or toys, please think of what your pet will enjoy, rather than what you would like to see it play with, and choose accessories with care, making sure you leave enough room for the hamster to exercise and burrow.

CHAPTER 4

FEEDING YOUR HAMSTER

1. Pre-mixed foods
2. Fresh foods
3. Treats
4. High-protein foods
5. Mashes and milky foods
6. Feeding guidelines

When you take home your hamster, remember that it is experiencing many changes – a new cage, the loss of its siblings, and a change of environment. Food is one area that you can, and should, keep the same – even though you may feel tempted to make changes. Keep to your hamster's established diet until it has settled in. Then, and only then, consider introducing a change of diet. We hear of so many newly purchased hamsters suffering tummy troubles, and when we inquire, "What have you fed them?", we find out that they have been fed every type of food mentioned in books. It is no wonder the hamster has an upset stomach – it has had too many new foods at once.

When you introduce new foods, do so gradually. Introduce a little of the new food along with the old, gradually changing the ratio until the hamster is eating the new food only. It should take a few weeks before your new hamster is eating the diet you choose.

A healthy hamster is one fed a well-balanced diet. Hamsters, like humans, enjoy a variety of foods, but it must be a nutritionally balanced variety. There are many types of food available, but you should take care not to overwhelm your hamster with too many choices that, together, are unlikely to form a nutritionally sound diet. Your hamster's diet should largely consist of a daily staple food, such as a dried, pre-mixed food. You can supplement this with fresh greens, high-protein foods, and milky or mashed foods. Your hamster will also appreciate the addition of treats to its diet, but these should be given sparingly.

1. PRE-MIXED FOODS

In the early days of hamster keeping, ready-made hamster mixes were not available. However, today, there are many mixes available, formulated to provide the hamster with all its dietary requirements.

A proprietary hamster mix, which may contain crushed oats, clipped oats, flaked maize, sunflower seeds, peanuts, dried peas, grass pellets, and some hard, dried biscuit, provides the hamster with its basic nutritional needs. Each individual proprietary mix is slightly different and may contain its own 'special' ingredients, such as dried banana, dried coconut, dried apple, or even an essence (e.g. raspberry) to flavour the mix. Whatever mix you use, all the ingredients take the form of hard foods, which, as well as being nutritious, are good for the hamster's teeth. Unlike human teeth, a hamster's teeth never stop growing, so it is vital that the hamster has the means to wear down its teeth by gnawing.

SAFETY FIRST

In recent years, there has been some concern over the quality and safety of some of the ingredients included in hamster mixes. In our experience, well-known manufacturers are usually the first to know about any likely problems with the ingredients in their foods and therefore take the appropriate action. A good-quality mix looks clean, fresh, and relatively dust-free, although some dust from the breaking of the ingredients is inevitable. Any whole oat grains should be clipped, i.e. there should be no sharp points on the ends of the oats.

Do not necessarily choose the cheapest mix you can find as hamsters can be very finicky about their food, and you may find that you throw more away than they eat. Also, some (although certainly not all) of the cheaper mixes may not have undergone the rigorous safety and quality checks of a more expensive brand. Remember that a few pence saved are not worth the life of your pet. Similarly, never use mixes formulated for other animals (e.g. rabbits and guinea pigs). Rabbit or guinea pig mixes are formulated for those particular species. At best, your hamster will not be receiving all the nutrition it needs. More seriously, the mix may contain ingredients that are dangerous to your hamster.

CHANGING THE MIX

Ideally, the first mix you buy for your new hamster should be the same as the one it was fed in the pet shop or by the breeder. However, if you are unable to establish what your hamster was fed prior to purchase, it is wise to use a standard mix for the first week or two, with no extras. Any new hamster we acquire is initially given a plain hamster mix (unless we know it is used to a daily supplement of a mash or milky food). Only very gradually do we introduce it to the extras of mashes, porridge, and greens, which most of our other hamsters enjoy as a matter of course.

If you know what mix your hamster received before you bought it, but you would still prefer to change to another, please remember to make the change gradually. As mentioned above, each mix is different, and although they may appear similar, a sudden change can still give your hamster an upset stomach.

STORAGE

Hamster mixes should be stored in an airtight container, to avoid contamination and to prevent the food from becoming damp. Damp hamster mix may start to grow mould, which, if ingested by the hamster, can affect the small capillaries supplying the extremities of the ears, tail, and feet, etc. In effect, this can cut off the blood supply to these extremeties. Always discard any mix that is damp or growing mould. When purchasing pre-mixed food, especially if it is sold loose as opposed to pre-packed, ensure that it has been stored in a covered, airtight container. Hamster mix sold from an open bag should not be stored where droppings, feathers, or other contaminates could fall in inadvertently. Many manufacturers now produce food that is pre-packed, which eliminates any possible contamination until it is opened.

2. FRESH FOODS
In their natural habitats, hamsters eat a variety of foods, and fresh foods are particularly enjoyed. You should try to emulate this for your captive hamster, who will greatly appreciate some additional foods, such as fresh fruit and vegetables.

All fruit and vegetables, whether wild or cultivated, must be fresh and frost-free. They should be washed thoroughly and allowed to drain prior to being placed in the cage. What your hamster enjoys, and how much it can eat without getting an upset stomach, will quickly become evident.

FRESH FRUIT AND VEGETABLES
Fresh greens are not a daily necessity for your hamster, but it will certainly enjoy them from time to time. Your hamster will probably like most of the vegetables you eat yourself, although, like humans, each hamster has its own individual tastes. Some of the greens you can try include broad beans, sprouts, broccoli, cauliflower, runner beans, cabbage, carrots, peas, sweetcorn, cucumber, bean sprouts and apple. All these foods should be given in small quantities only, e.g. a thin slice of apple *or* a slice of carrot *or* two or three bean sprouts, at any one time. Lettuce should be given very sparingly, as too much, too frequently, can be harmful.

Too much of any fresh food will result in your hamster developing diarrhoea, and, if the hamster tries to store the excess food, it will rot very quickly, making it unsafe to eat. Any uneaten fresh vegetables or fruit should be removed from the cage the next day.

Always remember that hamsters are very small, compared to humans. While humans can shrug off the effects of eating under- or over-ripe fruit and vegetables, a hamster may not. Always ensure that the fresh food you give is of good quality, perfectly ripe, has been well washed, and is given in small amounts.

WILD GREENS
Hamsters love wild greens. However, great care must be taken when collecting them to avoid any that have been contaminated by vehicle fumes or pesticides, or fouled by other animals. Thoroughly wash and dry any wild greens you collect to give to your hamster.

SUITABLE PLANTS
Dandelion (both leaf and flower), groundsel, clover, and watercress are normally enjoyed by hamsters and eaten with relish. Raspberry shoots are also enjoyed in early spring, and a small strawberry leaf can be beneficial if the hamster has loose droppings.

UNSUITABLE PLANTS
Buttercup, bluebells, bindweed, ragwort, elder, hemlock, speedwell and privet must be avoided, as they are poisonous to hamsters.

3. TREATS

Most pet shops sell a variety of 'treats' specially formulated for hamsters. Your hamster will greatly enjoy any treats you provide, but remember that they are treats, and should not be fed as part of the normal diet. Pre-packaged hamster treats range from a simple hamster yoghurt drop, to seed-coated sticks to be hung from cage bars. Chocolate drops are also available but the chocolate has a higher melting point than chocolate produced for human consumption. This ensures that the drops will not melt in the hamster's pouches. Under no circumstances should normal chocolate, including chocolate-coated biscuits, be fed to your hamster.

SIMPLE TREATS
You do not have to buy special treats from a pet shop for your hamster if you feel you would like to supplement its diet with some extras. Ours love the occasional piece of dried banana, peanuts in their shells, and sultanas. Raisins, a piece of plain biscuit, or some cooked potato are also popular. A millet spray, usually given to caged birds, also makes a great treat for your hamster on a special occasion. With the exception of pre-packaged hamster treats, and millet sprays for birds, make sure that any treats you intend to give to your hamster are suitable for human consumption – this will ensure that they are also safe for your hamster. Purchasing raisins, dried bananas, and peanuts from a specialist shop for humans ensures that our hamsters can enjoy their treats in safety. This may sound over the top but, as the old adage says, prevention is better than cure.

As hamsters put their food into their cheek pouches, sticky and sharp foods should be avoided. Sticky foods could adhere to the pouch lining, making removal difficult or impossible without veterinarian intervention, while sharp foods could cut or puncture the lining, allowing infection to set in.

SEED TREATS
Dwarf and Chinese hamsters will appreciate a smaller type of seed in addition to their basic diet. These include millet (either loose or on a spray), foreign finch seed and budgie seed. Syrian hamsters will also enjoy these seeds as an occasional treat.

4. HIGH-PROTEIN FOODS

Hamsters need a certain amount of protein to stay healthy. You can provide your hamster with extra protein in the form of a tiny amount of cooked chicken, or a little bit of scrambled or hard-boiled egg. The amounts given should be small, as any uneaten portion will spoil and foul the cage. Hamsters can also obtain extra protein from mealworms, which are normally fed live. Most hamsters will relish mealworms, and they are available from many pet shops, but if the thought of feeding live foods does not appeal to you, you can provide extra protein in some cooked chicken, etc. Today, many manufacturers have increased the protein content in their pre-mixed foods, so the provision of extra supplements is not always necessary. That said, however, you will find that your hamster will enjoy a small piece of chicken or ham occasionally.

5. MASHES AND MILKY FOODS

Bearing in mind the golden rule, that any new foods should be introduced gradually and in very small quantities, there are times when mashed or milky foods are beneficial to hamsters. Young hamsters, especially if raised with a milky supplement incorporated in their diet, will benefit from the extra calcium, which will help them to grow strong bones and teeth. A pregnant or nursing mother would also benefit. A hamster that is unwell, or one recovering from an operation or stroke, can normally be tempted to eat by offering a mash, porridge, or other milky foods, and these foods are also a good way to administer medicine to your hamster.

Elderly hamsters can greatly profit from supplements of milky foods or mashes. A lecturer from a nearby college, who brings students to our hamstery as part of their course, noticed how many of our hamsters were over two years old. After considering this, she concluded that our practice of feeding milky foods and mashes to our elderly hamsters contributed to their longevity, by providing them with easily digestible gluten (porridge oats), and milk to keep their teeth strong. Presently, one fifth of our hamsters are more than two years old, while a further fifth are more than 21 months old. Our ancient ones, as we call them, certainly do not look their age!

TEETH AND GUMS

Elderly hamsters will often put some of the hard, dry biscuits from their store into their mash or porridge to soften them. They will later be seen eating the soaked, softened biscuits, so we presume that, like humans, their teeth and gums deteriorate with age.

Mashes and milky foods also help if a hamster has pulled or loosened a tooth by snatching at the bars. Until the gum heals around the tooth, chewing hard food will be difficult and painful, but mashes and milky foods are easily consumed. Knoble, a beautiful, longhaired, satin copper male, somehow managed to pull out his top front teeth at the roots, at the age of seven months. He bled copiously for such a small creature, and the resulting black eyes had to be seen to be believed, but after a visit to the vet, he pulled through. For the rest of his long life, he lived on a diet of mashes, milky foods, and soaked hamster mix. He was also very forbearing about having his bottom teeth cut fortnightly. In all our years of hamster keeping he is the only one who managed to pull out his teeth in this way, although we have heard of several others.

SUITABLE FOODS

Our practice of cooking with very little salt means that any leftover boiled rice, spaghetti, boiled or mashed potato and other vegetables can be given to our hamsters in the form of a mash. Mashed or mixed with a little liquid (e.g. warm water, gravy, or meat juices), potatoes or rice are eaten with relish.

Hamsters love milk, but it is best not to give milk in its pure, liquid form. If it spills in the cage it will soak into the shavings and sour very quickly, making the whole cage smell unpleasant. Milk mixed with a cereal and allowed to swell usually stays in the hamster's food dish, and if it is spilt it does not soak into the shavings and will still be eaten. Runny porridge, a small piece of cereal biscuit soaked in milk, or a small amount of instant porridge made with milk, etc., are all suitable milky foods you can give your hamster. Cereals that are sweetened, honey-coated, or sharp, however, must be avoided.

HOW MUCH?

A small teaspoonful of a mash or milky food is ample for a single Syrian hamster. Quantities for Dwarf and Chinese hamsters should be smaller. If your hamster is not used to these supplements, feed tiny amounts to begin with, gradually building up to the teaspoonful.

You should not give your hamster mashed or milky supplements every day. Every two to three days would be sufficient, otherwise the hamster will probably eat the supplements to the exclusion of all else, leaving its pre-mixed food (or eating the choice bits only) and consequently failing to receive all its necessary nutrition.

6. FEEDING GUIDELINES

The main point to remember is that your hamster's diet should have a basic daily constituent that remains the same. Supplements and treats should remain just that – supplements and treats.

QUANTITIES

The guidelines given in this chapter apply to all species of hamster. However, if you own Dwarf or Chinese hamsters, consideration should be given to the size of the portion in relation to the size of the hamster. As a general rule, Dwarf and Chinese hamsters should be given smaller portions than their Syrian cousins.

All species of hamsters are hoarders, so somewhere in the cage there will be a pile of food (although the food dish may be empty). It is a good idea to check the size of the hoard each week, when you clean the cage. This will give you an idea of whether you are giving your hamster the right amount of food. Too large a hoard will encourage the hamster to eat its favourite foods only, so keep an eye on the hoard, reducing the amount of food you give if the pile seems to be increasing. Similarly, if there appears to be an absence of hoarded food, you are probably giving too little. Gradually increase the amount of food you provide until the hamster has a modest-sized hoard in the cage. Remember to check the hoard every week, to ensure you have not cut the rations down too much or to check whether further reductions are in order.

FADDY EATERS

At one pet hamster show we were judging, we were puzzled by the absence of any pre-mixed food in one cage. The cage was beautifully appointed with treats – half an apple suspended on string, a huge dishful of fruit and vegetables, and various honey-coated seed sticks hanging from the bars. When asked about the basic hamster mix, the owner replied that she did not give any as it was only left in a heap behind the nest. The hamster was a little thin and did not seem to have grown much, according to the owner. Three months later, on a diet of hamster mix and just the odd treat, the hamster was sleek, plump, and in excellent condition. If your hamster seems to pick at its food, choosing what it prefers rather than what it needs, you can encourage it to eat more sensibly by withholding treats and supplements. We do not give any pre-mixed food the day before we clean the cages, as this encourages our hamsters to root more deeply into their store and eat some of their less favourite items. However, always ensure that your hamster has access to food, and that it is not ignoring certain foods because they are past their best.

AFTER CLEANING
Uneaten food should never be returned to the cage after cleaning. If your hamster's food store is adjacent to the wet corner, it may be contaminated by urine. If the hamster has a house in which it sleeps, and it stores its food behind its nest, condensation will build up inside the house and on the dry food, which could then deteriorate from dampness. Any uneaten food you discover when you clean the cage should be discarded. However, be sure to provide more than the hamster's normal daily food allowance in the cage you have just cleaned – a newly cleaned cage does not have a hoard for the hamster to raid if it gets hungry.

CHAPTER 5

CARING FOR
YOUR HAMSTER

1. Handling
2. Cage cleaning
3. Grooming
4. Exercise and fun
5. Holidays
6. Escape and capture

As soon as your new hamster arrives home, it is best to place the hamster gently in the cage and leave it there, giving it time to explore its new home. If you have bought your hamster at the same time as the cage, and you bring them home together, make sure the cage is properly stocked and then leave your hamster in the cage for the rest of the day. A point to remember, if you are carrying your hamster's cage with your hamster inside, is that all hamsters can mistake fingers for food, especially if presented through the bars of the cage. When carrying a wire-topped cage with your fingers up against the bars, your fingers are easily accessible to the hamster, so it is worthwhile ensuring that your fingers are against the plastic base instead.

On the first day you have your hamster, you should talk to it softly, so that it is aware of your presence and becomes used to your voice. Do not handle it during this initial settling-in period, however, as it will have had enough disturbances for one day. A day is normally sufficient time for a new hamster to settle in.

Although hamsters are naturally nocturnal, and normally emerge to search for food around dusk, the rattle of food being placed in the food dish will rouse most. If you have a regular feeding time in the early evening or late afternoon, you will accustom your hamster to waking earlier, enabling you to enjoy your hamster more. When you feed your hamster, call out its name as it comes to investigate. You will find that your hamster quickly learns its name. Once your hamster regularly comes to your voice, you can, if you so wish, introduce a hamster house.

1. HANDLING

Do not expect your hamster to sit quietly on your hand the very first time you pick it up. Like all young animals, it will take time for your hamster to get used to you and to know what is expected of it. Over time, regular handling will ensure your hamster becomes tame.

The first time you try to handle your hamster, approach the cage quietly and talk to the hamster softly. Make sure your hamster knows you are there; if it is asleep in its nest, tapping the cage gently should wake it. Always wait until your hamster has emerged from its nest and is facing you before you try to pick it up. Be patient – removing it straight from the nest while asleep will almost certainly result in a bite from fright.

Please remember to make sure your hands are clean before attempting to handle your hamster. Hamsters rely a great deal on their sense of smell; if you have been eating sweets prior to handling your hamster, it may mistake your finger for a big sweet and take a nibble. Likewise, once you have finished handling your hamster and returned it to its cage, make sure you wash your hands thoroughly. No matter how clean you believe your hamster to be, thorough hand-washing is a hygiene necessity for hamster owners.

BITING

If your hamster bites you, it is a good idea to 'reprimand' it by giving it a very light tap on the nose with one finger while saying "No!" in a stern voice. Should a dog bite you, it would not be allowed to get away with it, and nor should your hamster. From experience, we have found that most hamsters learn quite quickly that biting is not acceptable.

THE TWO-HANDED PICK-UP

A new owner may have difficulty picking up a young hamster with one hand, especially as the hamster will probably make its way to the most inaccessible part of the cage. A two-handed pick-up is always advisable in the beginning, and, as many cages are not designed with this in mind, it is sometimes easier to remove the top of the cage. Place the cage in shallow cardboard box, approximately 4 inches (10 cms) deep and a little larger than the base of the cage. The cage top can then be removed with the knowledge that, should the hamster jump over the edge of the base, it will be confined to the cardboard box.

When your hamster is facing you, cup your hands gently underneath the hamster's body. Use a scooping action, never lifting the hamster more than 2 inches (5 cms) above the box or cage floor. Never restrain your hamster – if it wants to walk off your hands, let it. Repeat this a few times, encouraging the hamster into the box so that the base can be removed and the cage reassembled. If you spread your fingers slightly, it will not only make your hands bigger, it will also slow down your pet.

By placing one hand directly in front of the other, one after the other, it is possible to create a perpetual walkway for your hamster. You should then be able to encourage your hamster to walk across them. Never try to restrain your hamster at this stage. If it struggles and wants to go back to its cage, let it go. If you grip too hard you will frighten your hamster and it will almost certainly bite you.

When you first begin handling your hamster, you should do so for only a few minutes at a time. When you are ready to return your hamster to its cage, cup your

41

hands around its body and quickly but gently place it back in its cage. Giving your hamster a small treat will help it associate handling with something nice, and, given time, your hamster will look forward to being handled.

GAINING CONFIDENCE
Frequent but short handling sessions will help to give you and your hamster confidence in each other. As your confidence grows, try stroking your hamster gently while it sits on your hand, speaking quietly and reassuringly throughout. Avoid stroking the head, however, as this seems to make most hamsters nervous. If, at any time, your hamster wants to run from your hand, let it. Your hamster will quickly realise you intend it no harm, and it will soon be waiting to come out and be handled.

As your hamster becomes accustomed to you, you can increase the length of time it is handled. Some hamsters love to sit on your arm. Hold your arm against your body and let your hamster sit there. Keep your hamster secure, and safe from falling, by using your other hand to gently cup the hamster's body. You may find your hamster is so relaxed it goes to sleep there.

THE ONE-HANDED PICK-UP
When you are confident with the two-handed pick-up, try to pick up your hamster with one hand. Making sure your hamster's head is pointing towards your wrist, place your hand gently but firmly around its body, lift up your hamster, and put it on the palm of your other hand. Once you have mastered this, getting your hamster out of its cage will be relatively easy.

DWARF HAMSTERS
Although the handling procedures described above will work with all pet hamsters, it is worth remembering that, because of their size, a little more caution should be used when handling Dwarf or Chinese hamsters. Roborovski hamsters can be particularly difficult to handle because of their very small size and their incredible speed. When trying to handle these, use a larger cardboard box around the base of the cage. The box should be at least 12 inches (30 cms) deep, as Robos can jump surprisingly high. Chinese hamsters, on the other hand, can be extremely easy to handle once tame, because they have a tendency to hold on to your hands with their feet.

The Campbell has a reputation for being nippy, especially when being picked up. Consequently, you should always use your whole hand, rather than just your thumb and two fingers around the hamster's tummy, which must be uncomfortable for the hamster. Use the same type of pick-up with the Winter White hamsters. If you are keeping two or more together, always handle them both, so your scent is on both. You should try to handle your hamsters daily, even if it is just to pick them up and put them down again.

CHILDREN
Children should never be allowed to handle hamsters without appropriate adult supervision. Younger children may find it easier to sit in a chair and to have the hamster placed on their outstretched hands over their laps. Then, if the hamster is dropped, or if it decides to jump or run, it will come to no harm. The child must be

told to hold the hamster firmly, but very gently, as younger children can sometimes hurt a hamster without realising it.

2. CAGE CLEANING

You should clean your hamster's cage regularly, preferably once a week. If you keep a pair or colony in the same cage, cleaning may be required more frequently. While you clean the cage, your hamster should be put in a secure safe place, such as a play box (see below), an exercise ball, a plastic bucket, a small plastic tank, or even a spare cage.

All the shavings and food from the cage should be thrown away. Bedding need not be discarded automatically, but if it is soiled (looking or smelling dirty), it should be replaced. The water container should be emptied, rinsed, and filled with fresh water. If you use a water bottle, the use of a baby-bottle brush to clean the awkward neck areas will help prevent the build-up of green algae.

The cage should be washed with a cleaner formulated for animal cages, or with well-diluted washing-up liquid. After washing, the cage should be thoroughly rinsed and wiped dry. This will keep the cage looking and smelling fresh. Food dishes, wheels, houses, and toilets should also be rinsed and wiped dry.

Once you have washed and dried the cage, add clean shavings and place the bedding in the same area where it was prior to cleaning. Fill the food dish and water container, place them in the tank, and then return your hamster to the cage.

If you keep one hamster or two, you can dispose of the waste with your household rubbish. If you keep many hamsters and have a large amount of waste, you should check your local byelaws regarding waste disposal. It may be necessary to take the waste to special areas for disposal, if it cannot be buried or burned on your own property.

HEALTH CHECKS

Once you and your hamster have become accustomed to one another, and you are confident about handling your pet, consider giving your hamster a health check before placing it back in its newly cleaned cage. Even if you handle your hamster regularly, having a designated time for health checks means they are less likely to be overlooked. For example, Aberavon, a small rescued hamster of ours, loves coming out to be handled each night, exploring the sleeves of our jumpers, and so we reserve this time as handling time. At cage cleaning time, she is handled with her health and wellbeing in mind.

The health check should include looking at the coat and skin, stroking the fur to feel its condition, checking the ears for dry skin, looking for bar rub on the nose, and examining the brightness of the eyes. All these can be checked while the hamster is sitting on your hand.

The second phase involves looking at the hamster's underside. Some hamsters consider this an indignity, so it is best to accustom them to it from an early age. Pick up your hamster and position it so that its back is against the palm of your hand and your thumb is under its chin, leaving the rear end pointing towards your little finger. Ensure that you hold your hand so that the hamster's head is uppermost and its rear end is hanging slightly.

With the hamster in this position, it is relatively easy to see its chin, tummy, the genital area, the feet, and the toenails. Check for overlong toenails, lumps and bumps, dirty bottoms, and dribbly or wet chins. Overgrown teeth are usually obvious, but, should a hamster have a wet, dribbly chin, it could indicate that the teeth are overgrown. If you keep two or more Dwarf or Chinese hamsters together, use this weekly examination to check each hamster for bites as well.

You should not be holding the hamster firmly enough for a thorough examination of its teeth, or to cut its toenails, etc.; the weekly health check merely allows you to look for anything out of the ordinary. It is simply a way for hamster owners to keep a check that all is well or to spot a potential problem quickly.

3. GROOMING

Hamsters are fastidious about keeping themselves clean, so they will not normally need grooming. You can bring a shine to the coat of a shorthaired hamster simply by letting it run through your hands. If you have a satin Syrian hamster, you may find that the fur becomes greasy if it is handled for a long period of time. A small, soft baby brush works well for this, but it may take some time to accustom your hamster to it. With Chinese and Dwarf hamsters, grooming is not necessary.

LONGHAIRED HAMSTERS

Longhaired female Syrians need a little more attention, especially as they grow older. Although the fur does not get very long, tufts can grow around the rear end, which can become matted. The matting can be teased out using a fine comb. A cat's flea comb is ideal, but a soft baby brush or an old toothbrush is also suitable.

If you own longhaired male Syrians, with coats longer than 2 inches (5 cms), they may need special treatment if you wish to keep their 'skirt' – what people in the Fancy call the long hair on a male hamster – long and tangle-free. We find that the best way to keep the skirts of our males in top condition is to keep them on sawdust, rather than shavings. We use a coarse, plain sawdust, which is put through an old colander to remove any larger pieces that tend to act as 'curlers'. We used to groom daily, but found excessive use of the comb removed too much hair. Now, we groom our males twice a week, although we inspect them every day (when we feed them) for matting or tangles – if these are present we groom the hamster that night.

Young males should be accustomed to grooming before their skirt has fully developed. This will ensure that grooming does not become a problem when the hamster is older. Sit your young hamster on your hand, and give it a very quick groom. Over time, your hamster will accept this as a matter of course. The added advantage to beginning grooming at this young age is that the hamster will grow up to develop a very respectable skirt. Rogue, a longhaired, black-eyed cream hamster of ours proved that this technique works. At 18 months, his skirt was 5 inches (13 cms) long. He died at the age of 27 months, and during the last three months of his life we kept his skirt 3 inches (7 cms) long, so that he need not be troubled with regular grooming in his old age.

If your hamster has unmanageably long hair, which you find troublesome to keep tidy, you can trim the coat. Do not trim too much at one time, however, as this could lead to a chill.

Very longhaired males should not have a standard exercise wheel. Should the hamster's fur get caught around the spindle, it could trap the hamster in the wheel.

However, an alternative to the standard exercise wheel, which our longhaired hamsters greatly appreciate, is a cardboard roll (e.g. the insert from a toilet paper roll) suspended in the cage by wire. We also use extra-large wheels, with completely enclosed spindles, in the hamster's play boxes, for them to run on under supervision.

BATHING
Bathing can remove the natural oils from a hamster's fur, so we would not recommend bathing your hamster unless exceptional circumstances necessitate it. Even if you keep and exhibit white hamsters, they should not need bathing if they are kept correctly. However, from time to time, your hamster may get something particularly sticky or dirty in his fur, and the only way this can be removed is to bath the hamster.

Some time ago, a litter we had bred developed a slight infection and had to be put on antibiotics for a few days. The antibiotic, which was green in colour, was mixed in with their porridge. A short time after the porridge was put into their cage, the babies started to play-fight. Two of them were rolling around the cage, locked together in a mock fight, and they managed to roll into the bowl of porridge (now made green by the antibiotics). One of the hamsters became completely covered in green porridge, and as soon as we saw him a cry of "Oh, what a mess!" went up. We had to wash him twice before he was returned to his former glory, and from that day on his name has remained What-a-mess.

BATHING METHODS
It is best to use two bowls, each containing approximately 2 inches (5 cms) of warm water. This will save having to change the water while trying to hold on to a wet hamster. Always test the water temperature with your elbow, to make sure that it is not too hot.

Wet the hamster in the first bowl of water and then add a drop or two of baby shampoo to the hamster's fur. Rub in carefully, taking care to avoid the hamster's eyes. Rinse in the first bowl and then rinse again in the second bowl. Make sure that you have removed all the soap from the hamster's fur, and be careful that you do not lose hold of your hamster while bathing.

Once you have rinsed out the soap, place the hamster in a towel and dry carefully. You can finish drying with a hairdryer, but ensure that you keep one hand between the hairdryer and the hamster, so that the hot air does not burn the hamster. While the fur is drying, comb it carefully, to remove any tangles.

It is advisable to wash your hamster on a warm day or in a warm room, so that your hamster does not develop a chill. Make sure that the fur is completely dry before you put your hamster back in its cage, or the shavings will stick to its damp fur. It may be wise to let your hamster have a run in a play box for a few minutes, to help the fur to dry out.

4. EXERCISE AND FUN
Hamsters are renowned for disappearing into small spaces and gnawing anything and everything they find, so letting a hamster run free, however well supervised, can lead to problems. They have the ability to climb up inside furniture and squeeze into tiny spaces, and a gnawed electric cable is not only expensive to repair, it can also be very dangerous.

However big your cage may be, a hamster will greatly appreciate a change of scenery and the opportunity to 'run free' and explore. The two main options available are a hamster exercise or play ball, and a hamster play box.

EXERCISE BALLS

Like hamster wheels, exercise balls have caused some controversy among hamster owners. If you decide to buy one for your hamster, there are two main rules that should be followed, without fail.

• Never allow your hamster to remain in its ball for longer than 10 to 15 minutes (quite long enough to clean a cage).

• Make sure you supervise your hamster for the whole time it is in the ball.
   Exercise balls can easily become jammed under furniture, or may even burst open if the hamster runs straight into something. If the ball is being used on a carpeted area, check that the pile is not being nibbled through the air vents.

Some exercise balls can also be used on a stand, but the time limit is the same. Others come with an opening that allows the hamster free access to the ball on a stand, and these can be used as an alternative to a wheel in a cage. This type of ball is ideal to use in large tanks. Smaller versions of exercise balls are now available for Dwarf and Chinese hamsters, but the same rules of use apply.

Also on the market are some interesting variations on the standard hamster exercise ball. These include balls in the shape of cars and motorcycles, for example. However, bear in mind that these novelty balls are restrictive in size for a hamster, and may lead the owner, particularly younger children, to treat the hamster as a toy rather than a live pet.

PLAY BOXES

A simple way to give your hamster the opportunity to run free, both for your enjoyment and your hamster's, is to build a play box. This will not only give your hamster space to run around, but it will also ensure that it cannot cause damage or escape while doing so.

A simple play box can be made from a large cardboard box – the sort which a fridge or television comes in. It should be about 40 by 24 inches (100 by 60 cms) and approximately 12 inches (30 cms) high. The box can be held in shape using bulldog clips, so that it can be folded flat to store when not in use.

On its own, this box would be somewhat boring for the hamster, so why not make some toys to go in it. A large shoebox, with holes in the sides to enable cardboard tubes to be pushed in, makes a simple maze. Cardboard egg cartons, with a little food in each dimple, will keep your hamster exploring for some time. A clean, plastic drinks bottle, with a minimum size of 2 litres (3.5 UK pints/4 US fluid pints) makes a lovely tunnel once the top and bottom have been cut off and the edges sanded smooth. Commercially made toys can also be included, such as seesaws and plastic or wooden blocks.

When you place toys in the play box, ensure that none are too close to the sides, as this will enable your hamster to climb out. Although you can leave your hamster in the play box for some time, you should never leave it unattended for too long – cardboard can be chewed through in a matter of minutes, allowing your hamster an escape route.

Thick cardboard boxes will normally last for several weeks before needing to be replaced, even when used by litters. However, a cardboard play box used by a single hamster should last many months, although it may eventually look a little chewed. You will probably find that the corners are the first to be chewed, and one way to extend the life of the box is to place a large, washed stone in each corner, to prevent the hamster from accessing the corners to chew. However, make sure the stones are not too large, or the hamster will use them as stepping stones to the outside world. If you would like to make a more 'permanent' play box, a large, plastic storage box is ideal, although it cannot be folded flat for storage like a cardboard one.

5. HOLIDAYS

SHORT BREAKS

Hamsters can safely be left for two to three days, as long as they are given plenty of hamster mix, fresh greens, and water, and are placed out of direct sunlight. We normally provide our hamsters with some apple (approximately one sixth of the whole apple). Although the cut sides become dry and brown, the flesh inside retains plenty of moisture. If, out of boredom, the hamster decides to throw the water bottle from its cage, it still has access to moisture from the apple.

If the weather is hot, we draw the blinds in our hamstery, to keep the room cool. In cold weather, the heating is left on a timer so that the hamsters have no sudden drop in room temperature. You should also provide a little extra bedding in cold weather, in case of a heating failure.

LONGER HOLIDAYS

If you are away for more than a few days, you will need to make alternative arrangements for your hamster's care. Hamsters are excellent travellers, so, if convenient, you can take your pet with you on holiday. In this case, you should remove any accessories placed on a first or second level in a multi-storey cage, as well as the water bottle – every bump in the road will cause the water bottle to drip, so that, when you arrive at your destination, the water bottle might be empty and the shavings saturated. A piece of cucumber or apple will supply ample moisture for the duration of the journey. You should replace the accessories and water bottle when you arrive at your destination.

If you have a break during your journey, you will need to park in a shady spot, as the interior of a car heats up very quickly. Hamsters do not respond well to excessive heat or sunlight, so during the journey you should check that your hamster's cage is not getting direct sunlight through the windows of the car.

HAMSTER SITTERS

If you cannot take your hamster away with you, you will need to make alternative arrangements. If you bought your hamster from a local breeder, he or she may be willing to look after it for you. If this is not an option, you will need to find a hamster sitter. Ideally, this will be a person who has a hamster of their own, or someone who has kept hamsters in the past.

You should provide your hamster sitter with a contact telephone number for yourself (if at all possible), and the contact details for your vet, in case of emergency. You should also provide plenty of hamster food, and complete instructions for feeding (including what your hamster can or cannot have in the way of treats or greens, and how often).

If your hamster sitter is not experienced at handling hamsters, it is best to suggest that the hamster is not removed from its cage. It is far too easy for an inexperienced handler to drop a hamster, allowing it to escape. It is also worthwhile providing locks (in the form of bulldog clips) for the doors of your hamster's cage. Some hamsters are amazingly adept at opening cage doors, and you do not want to return home to find that your hamster is missing.

Always tell your hamster sitter if you have a mixed pair of Dwarf or Chinese hamsters, as there is the possibility of a litter arriving while the hamsters are in their care. We have received many desperate phone calls (via the RSPCA) from hamster sitters about this. Similarly, if your hamster is very old, tell your hamster sitter – if your hamster dies of old age while in their care, it saves them the agonies of wondering what they might have done wrong. With an elderly hamster, it would also be practical to let the sitter know of any special 'funeral' arrangements you might like, should the unthinkable happen.

Some years ago, we replaced a hamster that had died while in the care of a neighbour. After failing to persuade the neighbour to tell the hamster's owners the truth, we replaced the hamster with what we considered a good lookalike. A fortnight later we were contacted by the neighbour to let us know that all was well – the neighbour had even been congratulated by the child and the parents because the hamster was now very tame and loved to be played with!

6. ESCAPE AND CAPTURE
Hamsters, being naturally curious, will always seize the opportunity to set out to explore their surroundings. A weakness in a door catch, a door left open, a loose connection in a tubular cage, being left unsupervised during play – all these opportunities for escape are quickly exploited. All types of cages and tanks should be checked regularly for signs of wear or gnawing, which could lead to the occupants escaping.

DOOR CATCHES
One of the most common escape routes for an inquisitive hamster is the cage door. Some hamsters can open their cage door fairly easily once the cage has been in use for some time. We use a pair of pliers to re-bend the door catch to make it more secure, but a determined hamster can still manage to open the door. Therefore, we have resorted to putting a 'lock' on the door, i.e. a bulldog clip pushed over one side of the opening once the door is closed. We have found this to be the most effective type of 'lock' on a cage with bars, although there are other solutions – at a hamster show we once saw a cage with a small padlock on the door. This would work well in a household where younger children may try to open the cage unsupervised.

MODULAR CAGES
Some hamsters kept in modular cages have learned how to untwist the topmost module to escape. By lying on its back and twisting the top in the right direction, the hamster can unlock the top, push it off, and escape. We know of owners who resort to placing bricks or heavy books on the topmost module, to make it too heavy for the hamster to turn.

HAMSTER HOUSING

The cage should be
easy to clean, and
◀ have enough room
for eating, sleeping
and exercising.

Hamsters are lively
creatures, and enjoy ▶
the stimulation of
playing with toys.

A network of plastic
◀ tubes in the cage
will provide hours
of fun.

CORRECT HANDLING

To pick up a hamster safely, scoop him in your hands (above), and then place one hand over the top of him so he is held securely (below).

COAT CARE

Hamsters regularly groom themselves, but the longhaired ▶ varieties will need a helping hand.

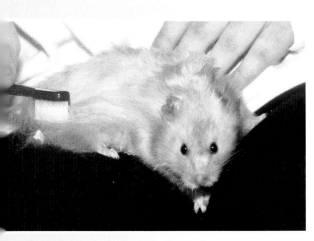

A toothbrush can be used to accustom ◀ your hamster to being groomed, and to remove shavings from the coat.

A small, metal comb is the most effective way ▶ of removing tangles.

A BALANCED DIET

A dry hamster mix is
◀ the best nutritional
diet to feed.

Some fresh treats, such
as cucumber, are eaten ▶
with great relish.

Remember, vegetables
and fruit can cause
◀ digestive upsets if fed
in excess, so should
only be given as
occasional treats.

A BALANCED DIET

Hamster cheek pouches can store ▶ huge amounts of food.

Hamsters often store their food to eat later. The ◀ hidden stashes should be removed regularly for hygiene purposes.

Water should always be available, preferably in the form of a gravity-fed ▶ water bottle and within easy reach of the hamster.

BREEDING HAMSTERS

A male Russian hamster.

A female Russian hamster.

In Dwarf breeds, such as the Russian hamster (pictured), both sexes take an active role in parenting.

BREEDING HAMSTERS

Ten-day-old Syrians –
the hair has started to ▶
grow, though the eyes
are still shut.

Sixteen days old –
◀ the hair is thicker
and the eyes are
now open.

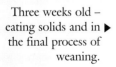

Three weeks old –
eating solids and in ▶
the final process of
weaning.

OUT AND ABOUT

A hamster will enjoy being let out of his cage to explore,
but do make sure the room is entirely safe and escape-proof
before letting him loose – and remember that some plants are poisonous.

A dig in a plant
pot makes an ▶
interesting change.

◀ Is it worth
attempting a climb?

An aerial view from ▶
the top of the plant.

CATCHING YOUR HAMSTER

Once free, hamsters can climb almost anywhere, drop down from elevated positions, and squeeze through the smallest of gaps. Many owners make the mistake of placing the hamster's cage (with the door open) on the floor, in an attempt to encourage the hamster back inside. This normally results in nothing more than the hamster removing its bedding and food from the cage and transporting them to its new den. While this means that the hamster is warm and well fed, it is still on the loose. The most effective way to capture an escapee is to use a bucket trap, which is successful nine times out of ten.

A tall bucket, set at a steep angle and propped up with books or bricks, with more books or bricks acting as a stairway to the top of the bucket, makes an excellent trap. If you use books, make sure they are not your favourites, as your hamster could collect more 'bedding' on the way and spoil your future reading. Adding some shavings, bedding, hamster mix, and some strong-smelling greens, will complete the set-up of this trap. The hamster is drawn to the food by its strong sense of smell. Broccoli and cabbage are quite odorous and are excellent for this purpose. The hamster will climb the 'stairs' and slide into the bucket to get to its prize.

Once inside, the hamster is unable to gain enough purchase on the smooth sides of the bucket (as long as the bucket is placed at a steep enough angle) to climb out again. The bedding, food, and the small amount of shavings will, therefore, encourage it to settle down to sleep without becoming too stressed by its inability to escape. A word of warning must be given at this stage, however. If you have a cat or dog, they must be restrained from entering the room in which the bucket trap is set up.

When you set a bucket trap, only use dried hamster mix or fresh greens, as other foods can cause problems. One young owner put her hamster's favourite food in the trap, only to find that she had caught a rat by the morning. On closer inspection, the rat turned out to be her beloved pet, completely covered in its favourite treat – peanut butter! The hamster then had to be bathed to restore it to its full glory.

Once you have captured your hamster, give it a quick check to make sure it has come to no harm during its adventure, and return it to its cage. Never forget to find the escape route your hamster used, and to take action to prevent a recurrence.

CHAPTER 6

COMMON PROBLEMS

Alphabetical listing of common, minor health problems

This chapter covers some of the health problems you may encounter during the daily feeding, or weekly cleaning, of your hamster and its cage. Not all ailments are listed because they are covered in chapter 9: A-Z of Hamster Diseases and Health Problems. Likewise, if you cannot find the answers to all your questions in this chapter, please refer to Section Two. This chapter is simply intended to answer the common queries that tend to worry first-time owners.

Many lesser health problems can be picked up relatively early, by noticing small changes in your hamster's attitude, movements, or appearance. By catching such problems early, you can prevent more serious complications from developing, and hopefully avoid the need for expensive, on-going veterinary treatment.

BAR RUB

This problem has faced hamster owners ever since hamsters were first kept as pets. When a hamster gnaws the bars of its cage continually, sliding its face up and down the bars as it does so, the result is an area of skin that is devoid of hair. In extreme cases, bar rub can lead to bleeding, which, in turn, leads to scarring on either side of the mouth or nose.

The most obvious way to stop bar rub is to give your hamster something else to chew, such as a commercial wood chew, or, for something different, you could try a small hide chew designed for dogs. You could also try putting a piece of fruitwood (e.g. apple) in the cage. If your hamster seems to gnaw in one particular place, try putting the piece of wood there. Unfortunately, some hamsters will continue to gnaw the bars whatever you do, and these may end up with permanently scarred faces. The only other alternative is to buy a plastic- or glass-tank cage.

COLDS
Strange though it may seem, hamsters can catch colds and flu from humans. In our household, anyone with flu or a bad cold avoids contact with the hamsters while infectious. A hamster with a cold may have rapid breathing, a wheezy chest, a cough, sneezing and spluttering fits, and even a runny nose. If your hamster displays these symptoms, isolate it from other hamsters and seek veterinary advice.

CUTS
Any cut on a hamster's body will bleed copiously. Bathe the cut gently with cotton wool (cotton) dipped in tepid water, and then assess the damage. Hamsters heal very quickly, so minor cuts and nicks can be left to heal on their own. Larger lacerations will need veterinary treatment, as will any wound showing signs of infection. Never feel tempted to use antiseptic creams formulated for human use.

DEHYDRATION
Hamsters can become dehydrated very rapidly, if they are subjected to sudden heat or a lack of water. Plastic- and glass-tank cages left in direct sunlight will intensify the heat, and, even if there is water available, the heat may overcome the hamster before it can drink. The same effect happens to hamsters left in cars during warm spells. Never leave your hamster's cage in direct sunlight, and ensure that your hamster's cage is always kept at the right temperature.

Another common reason for dehydration is due to the hamster's water bottle becoming blocked. Keep a daily check on the water level in the bottle. If it does not appear to be going down, check that the bottle is not blocked. You should also check the bottle for blockages every time the cage is cleaned. Holding the bottle in an upright position, run your finger over the ball-bearing in the spout. Your finger should become wet. If it does not, the bottle is blocked and you will need a new one.

A hamster that is suffering from dehydration will appear limp, as though in a deep sleep, and it will not react to handling. A hamster in this condition needs to be cooled and to have the water content in its body replaced very quickly. Try to encourage the hamster to drink, and remove it to a cooler area. Lightly spraying the hamster with cold water will sometimes help to reduce body temperature as well.

DRY EARS
You can hazard a rough guess at the age of your Syrian hamster by examining its ears. Youngish hamsters have hairy ears, while much older hamsters will have very little hair and their ears may appear shiny. Sometimes, with ageing, the skin on the ears will become flaky. If the flaky skin becomes thick and irritates the hamster, a little vegetable oil, baby oil, or petroleum jelly, rubbed between index finger and thumb and then rubbed gently over the ears, will help to relieve the flakiness temporarily.

DRY SKIN
The incidence of severe dry skin in hamsters seems to be less in recent years,

although it is not clear why. When we first started keeping hamsters, we had several that seemed unable to shed the topmost layer of dead skin. If the problem is not caught early, it can lead to a build-up of dead skin, which can crack and allow infection to set in, as well as causing the hamster irritation. When this happens, veterinary advice should be sought.

As they become old, very longhaired Syrian males will sometimes develop flaky skin (similar to dandruff), usually on the lower back. Regular grooming will help, especially if the hamster has become a little lazy and finds the long hair difficult to manage. We find that trimming the hair to half length can help, and it will soon grow back once the problem has been solved.

EYE PROBLEMS

BLINDNESS
Complete blindness is rare. Those we have seen have been 'Eyeless' (or Anophthalmic) Whites (page 142). As long as the cage furniture is kept in the same place, and the owner calls the hamster using vibration (e.g. tapping) and sound (e.g. voice), these hamsters cope exceptionally well. Braveheart, one such Eyeless White, pottered around his cage very happily and was very responsive to the human voice.

ENTROPION
Entropion is the term used to describe a condition in which the eyelid turns inwards, irritating the eyeball. It is seen mainly in rex (curly coated) Syrian and Dwarf hamsters. If your hamster develops this problem, seek veterinary advice.

FOREIGN BODIES
If the offending foreign body is not washed away by natural tears, and it remains in the eye, seek veterinary assistance.

'GUMMY' EYES
Generally, this is seen in older hamsters. One or both eyes will not open upon waking, but may open once the hamster has groomed itself. If not, a gentle wipe over, or bathing with lukewarm water and cotton wool (cotton), will moisten the closed eye and may help to open the eye or to encourage the hamster to groom around the eye.

LOSS OF AN EYE
Occasionally, a hamster will damage an eye so that it loses sight in that eye. In extreme cases of damage or infection, where there is danger of losing the eye, veterinary assistance should be sought.

Babies may sometimes lose an eye when a mother retrieves a wandering baby by grabbing the 'nearest bit' available. Nursing cats pick up their kittens by the scruff of their necks, but hamster mothers appear to pick up their babies any which way they can. Eyes lost or damaged early in life heal well, and hamsters seem easily able to compensate for the loss.

FALLS
Being short-sighted animals, hamsters are unable to perceive depth and height.

Consequently, it is all too easy for them to walk off the edge of a table and such like. Any fall can wind a hamster, and, even if no damage is done, the hamster can suffer shock from the fall. If your hamster suffers a fall, keep it warm and in a quiet place, allowing it time to recover from the shock before you try to assess the damage. Do not try to administer any stimulants or spirits, but seek veterinary advice if the hamster seems to have done more than just wind itself.

Some years ago, late at night, we were brought a hamster that had fallen off a high sideboard and knocked itself unconscious for more than 40 minutes. When the hamster arrived, he had a very large bump on his head and some blood in his fur. The owner left him with us and we put him in our heated recovery tank. The next morning, we took the hamster to the vet. The vet suspected that the hamster had fractured his skull, suggesting that we continued to keep the hamster warm and quiet in the recovery tank for a couple more days. Two days later, the bump had disappeared and the hamster was running around the tank like his old self. He was returned to his owners with instructions to restrict his mountaineering activities and he subsequently lived his full life span.

HIBERNATION

Strictly speaking, hamsters in their natural habitats do not go into complete hibernation. Rather, during the cold winter months, they may slip into a semi-dormant state during sleep. For captive hamsters, a sudden big drop in temperature, or a change in the circumstances in which the hamster is kept, usually triggers this type of 'hibernation'. Occasionally, we see newspaper headlines saying "Hamster Buried Alive" or "Hamster Back From the Grave", with the accompanying story of an apparently dead hamster returning to life.

At first glance, a hamster in this semi-dormant state appears dead. Breathing, heartbeat and temperature drop to such a low level that they are almost imperceptible. The hamster will also feel cool, or even cold, to the touch. Closer scrutiny may reveal the slightest twitch of a whisker, or tiny chest movements when a shallow breath is taken. In our experience, the 'hibernating' hamster is normally curled up out of the nest, as though overcome very suddenly.

Opinion is divided about allowing a hamster to remain in this semi-dormant state. Many people feel that hamsters kept in captivity are not physically prepared for such an eventuality. We would not allow our hamsters, spoilt and pampered after many generations of soft living, to continue for any length of time in this state.

If you find your hamster in this condition, place the hamster and its cage in a warm place, to allow its body temperature to rise. A warm hot water bottle (not overfilled), placed under the cage, is an alternative to a warm place. Usually, within half an hour, the hamster's breathing and heartbeat return to normal and the hamster will resume its usual routine soon afterwards. Add extra bedding and position the cage where the room temperature is constant, especially during cold spells, to avoid a repeat scenario.

HIP SPOTS

Syrian hamsters have two hip spots, one on each flank above the hip. These hip spots are scent glands, present in both female and male Syrian hamsters, although they are much more obvious in the male, the spots being much smaller on the female even when she is mature. In older shorthaired males, these two hip spots may become hairless, shiny, and quite conspicuous. This can worry first-time owners, because the spots were far less obvious when the animal was young. The male hamster has simply become sexually mature and is in good breeding condition. Male hamsters will expend a good deal of time grooming the two spots, which can result in them becoming even more obvious. The hip spots are not as visible on longhaired males, but in some colours the position of the hip spots is indicated by the 'gingery' appearance of the hair growing around that area. Both sexes may be observed marking their territory, by sliding or rubbing a hip spot against the side of the cage.

KINKED TAILS
This is often the result of a genetic fault or an accident. See page 113.

LUMPS AND BUMPS
Mysterious lumps and bumps are a source of panic for many owners, but many are quite normal and nothing to worry about.

TESTICULAR LUMPS
One of the most common causes of alarm for new owners is an increase in the size of a male hamster's testicles. As a young male matures, his testicles become more obvious. If he is warm, i.e. sleeping or being handled, they may become even more prominent. In this situation they may become highly visible, often for the first time, and this worries the owner. However, this is a normal state for the hamster and once he has been returned to his cage and allowed to cool down, his testicles will retract. However, should one or both testicles become distended, hard, or remain very visible without any retraction, seek veterinary advice, as there may be a chance of a testicular tumour. The exception to this is the male Chinese hamster, whose testicles are always fairly obvious, and this is nothing to worry about.

MAMMARY LUMPS
Mammary tumours are normally situated alongside or underneath a nipple. They may be quite firm to the touch, and they can grow very rapidly. If you suspect a mammary tumour, seek veterinary advice immediately.

Occasionally, a nursing female may develop mastitis, which may appear as swellings around the mammary gland area. Again, seek veterinary advice if you suspect this.

FACIAL LUMPS
A sudden enlargement of the face can normally be put down to the hamster gathering food or bedding in its pouches. However, if you notice that one or both sides of the face are continually 'swollen', some investigation may be necessary. You will need to watch to see if the hamster empties its pouch or pouches. If it does, all is well. If not, seek veterinary advice, because a pouch can become compacted and may need to be emptied under anaesthetic.

Alternatively, the hamster may have a tooth abscess or an infection, both of which will need veterinary attention.

DWARF HAMSTERS
Elderly Dwarf hamsters may develop soft lumps on the chest and tummy. Normally, these cause no problems, but should a lump become ulcerated, veterinary advice

should be sought. Removal of lumps in older animals is not always viable, as they may not survive the operation. The scent gland on the tummy of male Dwarfs can occasionally be confused with soft lumps (see below).

OTHER LUMPS

Some owners may think their hamster has a lump or bump that should be investigated, which then turns out to be harmless. For example, a plump hamster will appear to have bulges under its 'armpits' when it sits, which can appear quite alarming. However, the lumps will disappear when the hamster moves, and are nothing more than 'spare tyres' of fat. However, it is better to be safe than sorry, and the appearance of any unexplained lump should always be monitored carefully. Always seek veterinary advice if you are in any way concerned.

NAILS

A hamster that can exercise in a large cage, on an exercise wheel, or in a play box, very rarely suffers from overgrown nails. Overlong nails usually occur as the hamster grows older and less active, although Campbell and Winter White hamsters have a higher occurrence of long nails than Syrians.

If the nail has started to curl back on itself, it is too long and you will need to have your hamster's nails clipped. This can be done by putting your hamster on the top of its cage, and, using a small pair of scissors or a set of nail clippers, remove a very small amount from the end of the nail, just enough to take away the curve. This usually encourages the hamster to manicure itself, so that you do not have to. If you feel nervous about doing this procedure, ask your vet or your hamster's breeder to demonstrate for you.

NOISES

Hamsters are not normally considered to be vocal animals, but they can produce a surprising range of noises. Young or frightened hamsters will sometimes make shrieking sounds at the same time as turning on their backs in a defensive action. Female Syrian hamsters will sometimes call with a chirruping sound when they are on heat, and it is not unknown for a male to answer in the same manner. Elderly hamsters will produce what sounds suspiciously like snoring while asleep, and some even seem to dream, making a funny "mmmm, mmmm" noise. Dreaming is easier to spot in younger hamsters, where the mouth will be seen making eating motions at the same time as the noise is heard and the paws may also be seen twitching.

SCENT GLANDS

Campbell and Winter White hamsters have a noticeable scent gland on the tummy. When a hamster feels threatened or nervous it emits a foul smell from this gland, so presumably this is a defence mechanism against predators. In older, mature breeding males the gland can give the appearance of a large abscess or cancerous growth. It may look worrying but do not try to squeeze the gland or to treat it medically in any way. If you remain worried, seek veterinary advice.

STROKES

Yes, hamsters can have strokes. A hamster that has suffered a stroke will appear to rock backwards and forwards with each step when it tries to walk. You may also notice a rocking action while the hamster is lying in its nest. Occasionally, a hamster will lose the function of its limbs and become disorientated.

As with humans who suffer mini-strokes, recovery from a small stroke is usually quick, although other strokes may follow. If one of our hamsters suffers a stroke, we put it back in its nest, with food and water placed close by, and we monitor its recovery. Wedding, a Syrian hamster of ours, had a big stroke, but a week later the only outward sign was a slight limp in one of her hind legs.

TEETH PROBLEMS

If you feed your hamster the correct diet, and give it plenty of gnawing material, the chances of it developing any problems with its teeth are low. As the hamster grows older, its teeth take on a yellow tinge, but this is quite normal. The most common problems that occur are teeth that grow overlong, and broken or pulled teeth.

OVERLONG TEETH

As with all rodents, a hamster's front teeth continue to grow throughout the whole of its life. A hamster's teeth can grow surprisingly long, and many owners, on seeing their hamster's teeth for the first time, may assume that the teeth need clipping. It is very difficult to say how long a hamster's teeth should be, as this is dependant on the hamster's overall size. Therefore, it is easier to look for symptoms that indicate overgrown teeth.

A hamster that regularly chews the bars of its cage may have overlong teeth. A hamster that loses weight, because discomfort from its teeth prevent it from eating, may also have overlong teeth. Other symptoms include marks around the mouth, and/or blood around the mouth, as overlong teeth may lead to the hamster accidentally injuring itself. Left untreated, overlong teeth may lead to more severe problems, such as tooth breakages or loss.

The best way to avoid the problems caused by overlong teeth is to prevent the teeth from becoming too long in the first place. Make sure you provide ample material for your hamster to gnaw on in its cage. Trying to clip your hamster's teeth is not an easy task and should not be attempted by the novice. Most hamsters will not sit quietly while you try to get a small pair of scissors or nail clippers in their mouth, and the possibility of nicking your hamster's tongue, or even a paw, is very high. If you feel your hamster's teeth need clipping, take it to the vet, who will assess the teeth and clip them if necessary.

BROKEN OR LOST TEETH

While your hamster needs plenty of gnawing material to keep its teeth in check, gnawing hard objects such as cage bars, hard food, or wooden gnaws, can result in your hamster breaking a tooth. Blood in or around the mouth could indicate a broken or pulled tooth, while sudden loss of weight is another indication that something could be wrong with the teeth (although it may be that your hamster is simply unwell).

If your hamster breaks or loses a tooth, the corresponding upper or lower teeth will have nothing to bite against, so they will continue to grow unchecked, possibly to the point where they will grow into the opposite gum. If you suspect any problems with your hamster's teeth, seek veterinary advice immediately.

If your hamster loses a tooth, or a set of teeth, completely, not only will the remaining teeth need continual clipping, but your hamster's diet will also need to be adjusted. Your vet will clip the hamster's remaining teeth, and will train you to do this yourself, if need be. Feeding soft foods (e.g. porridge, boiled potato, mashes of various kinds, or even second-stage baby foods) will let the hamster eat without too much discomfort, and most hamsters with missing teeth live their normal life span.

THINNING FUR

This is usually associated with older hamsters. Often, the fur will become thinner and the belly may become completely bald. Alternatively, the hamster may lose patches of fur from a flank or limb. The remaining fur will be thick and normal. As with humans, baldness is not inevitable; some old hamsters will lose fur whereas others will not. Thinning fur may also be seen in nursing females. A female who has just raised a litter may lose fur on her flanks, but once she is back in good condition the fur normally grows back.

TWIRLING

Twirling refers to a condition in which a hamster turns round and round on the spot, or runs around in small circles. If the condition manifests itself suddenly, it may be due to an inner ear infection, which a course of antibiotics from the vet can treat. If the condition is seen in very young animals, the probable cause is some sort of brain damage, which is unlikely to be treatable but is probably not life-threatening. We had one hamster that ran in circles (although not very tight circles) but would stop immediately if distracted by food. He could be handled very happily, and although he was not particularly long-lived, he saw his first birthday and died quietly in his sleep.

URINE CHANGES

A noticeable change in the colour of your hamster's urine may indicate health problems, so you should keep a regular check on the colour of your hamster's 'wet corner'. If the shavings in this corner change colour, it may be a symptom of a urine infection. However, it could also be the result of using different shavings, which, when wet, turn much darker than those previously used. Dietary changes may also affect the colour of the urine. We once gave our hamsters beetroot, which resulted in all the wet corners having a reddish tinge and us having small heart attacks! If all external possibilities are eliminated and the problem persists, and especially if your hamster looks under the weather, consult a vet.

WEIGHT LOSS

Any sudden, noticeable loss of weight could be an indication that all is not well with your hamster's health. If your hamster is losing weight, the first thing to check is its teeth, to make sure your hamster has not stopped eating because it is in discomfort from broken or overgrown teeth. If you find nothing obviously wrong with your hamster's teeth, check its water bottle by stroking the ball-bearings in the spout to see if the water will flow. If the nozzle is blocked, your hamster could be dehydrated, especially if the weather is hot. Most hamsters will normally lose weight as they age, but weight loss is usually very gradual, not sudden. If you are worried about your hamster's weight, monitor it closely, and, if any signs of illness occur, or if you are at all worried about the weight loss, seek veterinary advice.

CHAPTER 7

ANATOMY AND PHYSIOLOGY

1. The skeleton
2. The sense organs

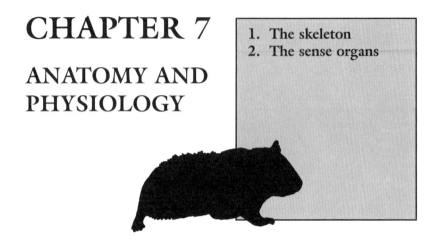

The 26 species and subspecies of hamster belong to the rodent family. All hamsters are small, 'stubby' animals, with short legs, a blunt nose and a stubby tail. The tail, ears and feet have a thin covering of fine hair, while the rest of the body is covered with dense, soft fur. The average life span for a hamster is 18 to 36 months, although there are recorded cases of hamsters living much longer than this. The normal body temperature of a healthy hamster is 37 to 38 degrees Celsius (98.6 to 100.4 degrees Fahrenheit).

1. THE SKELETON

SKULL AND JAWS

With the exception of the lower jaw, the skull is made of many flat bones that are joined together by fibrous tissue with little or no movement between them. The lower jaw consists of two bones, the left mandible and the right mandible. Unlike many other species, these two mandibles are not fused where they meet at the front. This allows each mandible to move slightly within the gum. The joints where the mandibles articulate with the upper skull are elongated horizontally, which allows the jaw to slide forwards and backwards. When the hamster picks up food, or is gnawing, the front teeth are aligned but the back or cheek teeth are not. The jaw moves backwards when food is chewed, allowing the back teeth to be used

Skull And Teeth

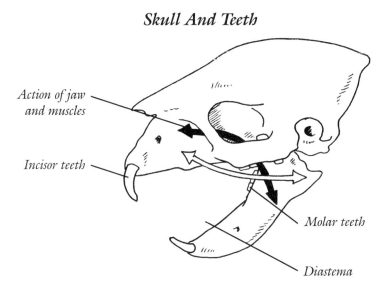

Action of jaw and muscles

Incisor teeth

Molar teeth

Diastema

effectively. However, when this happens, the front teeth are no longer aligned, so the hamster cannot gnaw.

TEETH

Hamsters have a total of 16 teeth – a pair of incisors on either side (four in total), and three pairs of molars or cheek teeth (12 in total). The incisors are curved and deeply embedded in the jawbone, so that most of the tooth is below the surface. The inside of each incisor contains highly sensitive tissue known as the pulp cavity. This is surrounded by a harder substance called dentine. The front side of the tooth (i.e. the side nearest the lips) is further protected by enamel, both above and below the gum line, while the inner side of the tooth is protected by a substance known as cement. Enamel contains a yellow-orange pigment that is evident from about 16 days old and becomes darker with age. This normal coloration should not be mistaken for disease or decay. Enamel wears more slowly than cement or dentine, so the incisors naturally form a sharp edge along the front.

The roots of the four incisors are permanently open, which is why the incisor teeth continue to grow throughout a hamster's life. If they are not worn down because they do not meet properly (see Malocclusion, page 100), they will keep growing, eventually curving round and causing difficulty eating. If the teeth are not clipped, they will eventually block the mouth or grow into the opposite gum.

Hamsters do not have canine teeth. The toothless gap between the incisors and the back or molar teeth is called the diastema. The lips and cheeks bulge inward through the diastema, separating the gnawing area of the incisors from the molar region.

The molar teeth are used for crushing and chewing food. Some molars have open roots but this is not always the case. Consequently, malocclusion resulting from overgrown back teeth is less common. However, a hamster's molars can suffer from dental caries and decay, usually caused by food particles retained in the molars.

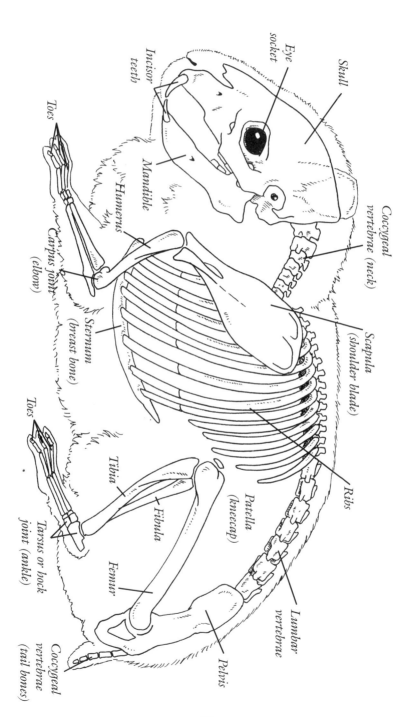

Eye socket

Incisor teeth

Skull

Coccygeal vertebrae (neck)

Toes

Mandible

Humerus

Carpus joint (elbow)

Sternum (breast bone)

Scapula (shoulder blade)

Ribs

Toes

Tibia

Fibula

Femur

Patella (kneecap)

Lumbar vertebrae

Tarsus or hock joint (ankle)

Pelvis

Coccygeal vertebrae (tail bones)

68

SPINE AND TAIL

The spine consists of individual bones called vertebrae. Each vertebra has a hole in the middle, which lines up with the holes in other vertebrae to form the vertebral canal. The hamster's spinal cord runs through the vertebral canal, the delicate nerves of the spinal cord being protected from damage by the hard, bony casing of the vertebrae.

A hamster's spine consists of five different types of vertebrae. The first seven vertebrae, which are known as cervical vertebrae, form the neck. The first vertebra of this section articulates with the skull and is called the atlas.

The second type of vertebrae are known as thoracic vertebrae. These 13 bones have a rib attached to either side, forming the hamster's chest area. The front ribs join the sternum (breast bone) at the bottom. The back ribs, which are known as floating ribs, do not attach, allowing the rib cage to move in and out for breathing.

Along the loins are six lumbar vertebrae and four sacral vertebrae. The sacral vertebrae, which usually fuse in adults, join the pelvis at the sacroiliac joint. Continuing on from the sacral vertebrae are the bones that make up the tail. Although hamsters have extremely short tails, there are 13 to 14 tiny vertebral bones in the tail. These are known as the coccygeal or caudal vertebrae.

LIMBS

Hamsters have short legs with small bones. Due to their small size, these bones are susceptible to fracture, particularly in overweight individuals or a hamster fed a diet low in calcium.

2. THE SENSE ORGANS

THE MOUTH

Hamsters have two noticeable characteristics in the mouth – the cheek pouches and the upper lip. The upper lip is cleft (i.e. it does not meet in the middle), so the incisors are visible even when the mouth is closed.

The buccal cheek pouches are probably the most well-known characteristic of the hamster, from which it takes its name (the name hamster is derived from the German word 'hamstern', meaning 'to hoard'). They are usually used for storing and transporting food, although females may hide a newborn litter in their pouches if they are disturbed. This is not an ideal hiding place, however, as the babies may suffocate.

The cheek pouches are actually muscular sacs. They can enlarge to a considerable size, extending on each side of the head and neck as far back as the shoulder. They are formed from the mouth in the diastema region, and open just behind where the lips and cheek bulge inwards. The pouches have no lymph supply, which means that the cells of each pouch do not recognise foreign material. Very dry or sticky food will sometimes become stuck (see Impacted cheek pouches, page 97), causing an alarmingly large swelling on the side of the head and neck.

THE EYES

Hamsters are short-sighted. They can be easily startled if they do not see an approaching object, which is why some hamsters have a tendency to bite. The eyes are normally dark (albinos are an exception) and are situated on top of the head, giving a good all-round view of possible predators. Each eye consists of a delicate globe protected by a bony socket. Most of the globe is contained inside the socket, and only a small part of the eye is visible on the outside. The true size of the eye can be seen in the unfortunate event of a prolapse of the eye (see page 93).

Each eye has a top and bottom eyelid, and a third eyelid in the inner corner, called the nictitating membrane. Dehydrated hamsters will have a far more prominent nictitating membrane. The eyelids are lined with a mucous membrane called the conjunctiva, which becomes red and swollen when irritated (see Conjunctivitis, page 88). The third eyelid contains the Harderian glands. These are pigmented (dark-coloured) in females but non-pigmented in males. These glands also produce fluid (i.e. tears) to lubricate the eye surface, as does the lachrymal gland, situated under the top eyelid. Tears are drained from the eye by ducts in the inner corner, which open to the nose. Irritants, such as smoke, cause an increase in tear production. Excess tears overflow from the eye (i.e. crying), while the rest run out of the nose. Excess tear production from the eyes and nose is a symptom of various allergies.

The eye is held in the socket by muscles that can rotate it slightly to alter the area of vision. It is filled with fluid called the humour, which supplies nutrients to the internal structures, and is constantly produced and drained out of the eye. Any alteration in production or drainage results in swelling caused by too much fluid, which is termed glaucoma (see page 95).

The surface of the eye is called the cornea. A healthy cornea is clear, allowing light to enter the eye and focusing it so that it passes to the back of the eye, which means that the hamster can see. The iris is a coloured muscle inside the eye (black in hamsters), with a hole in the middle called the pupil. The iris alters the size of the pupil to allow a constant amount of light to the back of the eye. In dim light the pupil will widen, whereas in bright conditions the pupil will shrink.

The lens is a solid structure in the middle of the pupil that can change shape to focus light on to the back of the eye (the retina). The lens is usually clear, but it can become cloudy, due to cataracts. Cataracts reduce the lens's ability to allow light through the eye and to accurately focus it to create vision (see page 88).

The retina is the camera of the eye. It has a good nerve and blood supply and converts light rays to nerve impulses. These impulses leave the eye via the optic nerve, situated at the back of the eye. The optic nerve channels the nerve impulses to the opposite side of the brain where a visual image (picture) is produced.

THE EARS

The ear is an organ of sound and balance divided into three parts. The external ear has a flap called the pinna (which is large and rounded with a thin covering of fine hair on the surface) and a passage or external canal (which leads down into the middle ear). The pinnas are pricked and pointed when the hamster is alert, helping to divert sound waves down the ear canal. A drooping pinna can be a sign of middle ear infection. There is normally little earwax in the ear canal. If wax is visible, particularly if it is dark in colour, this may suggest an ear mite infection (page 92).

The external and middle ears are separated by the eardrum, which can rupture in severe infections or if pierced by a foreign body (e.g. a bit of straw). There are three bones in the middle ear that transmit sound waves further into the head. The middle ear also connects to the pharynx (the back of the mouth) via the eustachian tube.

This allows air out to reduce pressure, but it can also let in infections, which is why middle ear infections often follow a respiratory infection.

The inner ear is a delicate structure deep inside the temporal bones of the head. It has structures to convert sound waves into nerve impulses and to send them to the brain. Part of the inner ear is involved in balance, so infections of the inner ear can cause problems with balance, such as circling and head tilt (see page 96).

THE NOSE

Being short-sighted, smell and touch are particularly important to hamsters exploring the environment and looking for food. The nose has a plentiful blood and nerve supply, making it particularly sensitive. There are several long whiskers on the end of the nose, which are used to sense objects in the environment.

THE SKIN

Hamsters have a large amount of thin, loose skin covered with dense, short fur. The skin is firmly attached to the underlying muscle in the breast-bone area, but elsewhere it can be extensively moved or stretched. Fortunately, this means that large wounds can be closed and generally heal well after repair or surgery.

There are sebaceous glands on both sides of the flank. These show as dark-brown patches with coarser hair. They are more developed in males. They are fully formed by 21 days in females and 70 days in males. They are used to mark territory and are involved in mating behaviour – a sexually active male will have wet flank hair from the secretions of these glands. The male hormone testosterone is converted to dihydrotestosterone in the sebaceous glands, and, when active, the secretions are thought to attract females.

The skin surrounding the shoulder-blade area covers brown-coloured fat deposits. These deposits are stored by hamsters to provide energy. The fat is burned off to provide heat, which is essential for newborn or hibernating hamsters.

CHAPTER 8

MAJOR BODY SYSTEMS

1. Respiratory system
2. Cardiovascular system
3. Digestive system
4. Endocrine system
5. Urinary system
6. Reproductive system

1. RESPIRATORY SYSTEM

The purpose of the respiratory system is to exchange gases in the hamster's lungs, so that the blood receives an adequate supply of oxygen to feed the cells that make up the hamster's body.

The respiratory system is basically an airway system, running from the hamster's nostrils to the depth of its lungs. It consists of an upper and lower section. The upper section includes the nose, throat, and trachea (windpipe), while the lower part includes the lungs, consisting of the bronchi, bronchioles, and lung tissue. Hamster lungs are divided into five parts, known as lobes. The left lung consists of one whole lobe, while the right lung is made up of four lobes.

UPPER RESPIRATORY SYSTEM

The upper airways transport air to the lungs. Air is breathed in through the nose or mouth, and travels down the trachea to the lungs. The nose and windpipe contain fine hairs, called cilia. These act as a protective feature, trapping small particles of dust and disease and preventing them from entering the lungs. In the trachea, the cilia have the ability to move, steadily pushing a covering layer of mucus (and any trapped particles contained therein) back up to the throat. Extra mucus is produced in response to the irritation, which then causes the hamster to cough up the offending particles, or to discharge them from its nose. Many healthy hamsters have

72

Lungs, ventral view

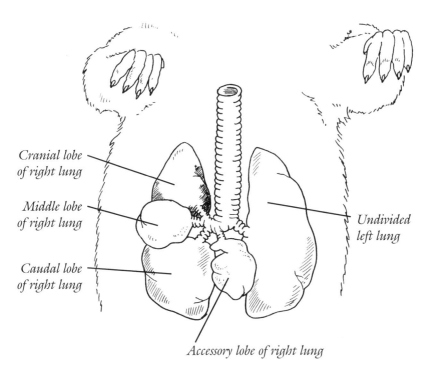

Cranial lobe of right lung

Middle lobe of right lung

Caudal lobe of right lung

Undivided left lung

Accessory lobe of right lung

bacteria present in their throats as a matter of course. Normally, these bacteria stay in the throat and do not cause problems. However, when the cilia or mucus become disrupted through irritation, the bacteria in the throat can sometimes enter the lungs and cause pneumonia.

Right at the back of the hamster's throat, at the top of the trachea, there is a moveable flap called the epiglottis, which covers the entrance to the larynx (voice box). The epiglottis is normally open, which allows the hamster to breathe. However, it closes when the hamster swallows or when the larynx is touched, to prevent foreign material (e.g. food) from entering the lungs. When the hamster swallows food, the epiglottis is closed and food is directed down another pipe (the oesophagus) to the stomach.

The trachea, which channels air into the lungs, consists of a series of cartilage rings. In hamsters, these rings are not uniform in size and shape as they are in many other species; some of the rings are split or 'V' shaped. This does not seem to be of clinical significance, however, and the rings are unlikely to collapse and cause the hamster difficulty when breathing.

LOWER RESPIRATORY SYSTEM

The trachea is the windpipe that channels air into the lungs. At the bottom, the trachea splits into two bronchi, one entering each lung. Airways called bronchioles branch off from the bronchi, and end in tiny, thin-walled sacs called alveoli. The alveoli form part of the lung tissue, and they are responsible for infusing oxygen into the blood and removing waste products.

When oxygen enters the alveoli of the lungs, it passes through the thin cell walls and enters the bloodstream. When oxygen enters the blood, the blood is forced to release the waste product of carbon dioxide, which travels back through the alveoli cell walls. The hamster breathes out the carbon dioxide, and the process is repeated.

The chest area, known as the thorax, is separated from the abdomen by a powerful muscle called the diaphragm, which plays an important role in the hamster's breathing. When the hamster breathes in, the diaphragm flattens and the ribs move outwards, to allow the lungs to expand with air. This is why the hamster's back ribs are so-called floating ribs, because they allow the chest to expand when the hamster breathes.

A hamster's respiratory rate is variable, between 35 and 135 breaths per minute. The rate will increase if the hamster is suffering from disease or pain, and it will become very shallow and slow in a hamster that is hibernating. Indeed, the respiratory rate of a hibernating hamster can become so slow and shallow that it is barely noticeable. This is why it is not uncommon for an owner whose hamster is hibernating to believe that the hamster is dead.

2. CARDIOVASCULAR SYSTEM

The cardiovascular system consists of the heart, arteries, and veins. Its role is to transport oxygenated blood to the hamster's vital organs. Oxygen is essential for cells (the basic building bricks of all body tissues) to function.

At the centre of the cardiovascular system is the heart, a powerful muscular pump situated in the thorax (chest), between the lungs. It consists of four chambers – the left and right atria and the left and right ventricles – and pumps blood around the body continually, for the whole of the hamster's life.

For descriptive purposes, the circulatory system begins in the heart's right ventricle. When the ventricle contracts, blood is forced out of the heart to the lungs. The blood collects oxygen and deposits carbon dioxide through the single-celled walls of the alveoli (see above). The oxygen-rich blood then returns to the left atrium, which then contracts, forcing blood through a one-way valve in to the left ventricle of the heart. Once the left ventricle becomes full, the valve shuts, ensuring that blood flows in one direction through the heart and around the body.

When the newly oxygenated blood reaches the massive left ventricle, it is pumped into a major vessel called the aorta. The left ventricle is six times as thick as the right, because of the greater muscular pressure needed to pump blood all round the body. The aorta branches into many arteries, which transport the oxygenated blood to the cells that make up the hamster's vital organs. The cells remove the oxygen from the blood, and deposit their waste of carbon dioxide back in the blood. The 'used' blood is returned to the heart through veins, which flow into larger, major veins called the vena cava. Hamsters and other members of the rodent family are unusual among mammals because they have three vena cava, rather than the 'normal' two.

The vena cava empty into the right atrium of the heart, which acts as a collecting chamber for blood returning to the heart. When the atrium becomes full and contracts, blood is forced into the right ventricle and the process begins again.

BLOOD

The blood volume of a healthy hamster, as with all mammals, is 8 to 9 per cent of its bodyweight. Blood supplies the various tissues and organs of the body with everything they need to function, as well as removing the toxins (poisons) they produce. It is made up of white blood cells, red blood cells, and platelets suspended in a watery fluid called plasma. Red blood cells carry oxygen to the cells, while white blood cells form part of the immune system, helping to fight infection. Platelets are involved in sealing wounds and helping blood to clot. Plasma also contains many important nutrients and chemicals.

Hamsters have unusual white blood cells. They have a tendency to produce amyloid, an abnormal protein, probably produced as the result of an overactive immune response. If amyloid is deposited in the major organs, it can cause severe damage, contributing to heart, kidney, and liver failure.

HEART PROBLEMS

Heart problems are common in elderly hamsters. Many are caused by blood clots, which block the blood supply throughout the body (known as thrombosis). Another common cause of heart problems is muscle degeneration in the heart. This makes the heart much weaker, which means less blood is supplied to the lungs, and, therefore, less oxygen is sent round the body. The brain responds to any reduction in oxygen by telling the heart and lungs to work faster, which is why affected animals puff and pant, although if the brain is seriously deprived of oxygen, the hamster will collapse and die.

The heartbeat can be felt with a finger and thumb, placed either side of the hamster's chest just by the elbow. The normal heart rate is very fast, from 250 to 500 beats per minute, which makes it difficult to count and impossible to tell if it is raised.

3. DIGESTIVE SYSTEM

Digestion is the process by which food is broken down into small, nutrient-rich particles. The digestive system absorbs nutrients from food, passing them into the bloodstream. The blood then transports the nutrients to the body's cells.

The hamster's digestive system is adapted for a varied diet with a high grain content. The large intestine conserves water, as would be expected in an animal originating in desert conditions.

MOUTH

The digestive process begins in the mouth, when the hamster uses its cheek teeth to grind up food. Several glands – known as the submaxillary, parotid and sublingual salivary glands – produce saliva, which lubricates food to make it easy to swallow. Saliva also contains some enzymes that help to break down the food into smaller particles. Once the food has been swallowed, it passes to the stomach via a tube called the oesophagus.

STOMACH

The stomach of a hamster is divided into two separate parts. The first, or fore stomach, has a higher pH level, making it less acidic than the second stomach. The fore stomach contains microbes (bacteria) that aid digestion of fibrous material, such as hay. This is similar to the rumen (first stomach) of cattle, sheep and goats, which also have more than one stomach. Some fermentation of food also takes place in the fore stomach.

The second part is called the glandular stomach, which is similar to the simple stomach of non-ruminants, such as humans, dogs, cats, and pigs. The glands in this stomach produce acids and enzymes to digest the protein in the diet. The muscular

Gastrointestinal tract

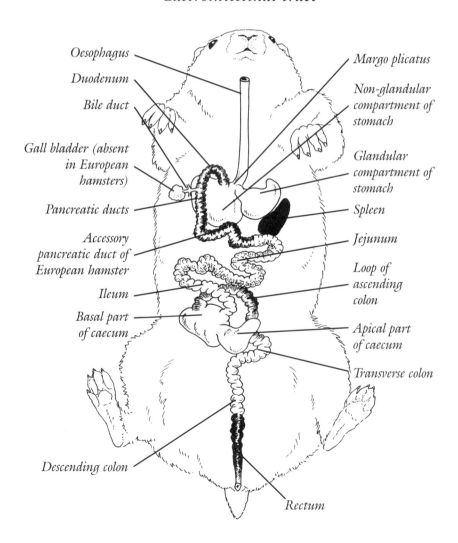

Oesophagus

Duodenum

Bile duct

Gall bladder (absent in European hamsters)

Pancreatic ducts

Accessory pancreatic duct of European hamster

Ileum

Basal part of caecum

Descending colon

Margo plicatus

Non-glandular compartment of stomach

Glandular compartment of stomach

Spleen

Jejunum

Loop of ascending colon

Apical part of caecum

Transverse colon

Rectum

walls of the stomach contract, churning up the food and mixing it with the enzymes.

Food stays in the stomach for a few hours before it passes into the intestines. This is to give the enzymes time to break down the food. By the time the food leaves the stomach, it has an even, soup-like consistency.

SMALL INTESTINE

The small intestine is a long, coiled tube divided into three sections, the duodenum, the jejunum, and the ileum. It is here that most food digestion and nutrient absorption takes place.

The role of the small intestine is vitally linked to the pancreas and the liver. The pancreas is an organ lying close to the duodenum. It produces a variety of enzymes that are emptied into the duodenum via a small tube or duct. Bile is also emptied into the duodenum via the bile duct, which stems from the gall bladder of the liver. Bile contains substances that help to break up fat. The enzymes and bile in the duodenum digest a large percentage of the food eaten by the hamster.

Food passes from the duodenum to the jejunum, which is the longest part of a hamster's small intestine, measuring approximately 10 inches (25 cms). Digestion is completed in the jejunum and absorption begins. Digested particles are absorbed through the gut lining into blood vessels, which transport the particles to the liver.

Absorption continues in the ileum, the shortest part of the small intestine, measuring less than 0.8 inches (2 cms). Nutrients are absorbed the same way as in the jejunum, travelling through the gut wall and into the liver. Once the nutrients have reached the liver, they are stored until needed or modified. If modified, they will be used as 'building blocks', providing energy and growth for the body's cells.

LARGE INTESTINE

The large intestine is composed of the caecum, the colon, and the rectum. The caecum and colon are large and adapted to conserve water. The caecum is a blind ended structure, with a separate entrance and exit close to each other called the ileo-caeco-colic junction. Material enters from the ileum and exits to the colon.

The caecum is responsible for digesting plant fibre known as cellulose, as well as producing vitamins B and K. Unlike the small intestine, which absorbs nutrients from digested food matter, the caecum does not absorb the vitamins and nutrients it produces. Instead, the nutrients are formed into small, soft pellets, which are excreted from the body via the colon. The passing of these soft pellets triggers an immediate response in the hamster's brain, and it will hunch over to eat the pellets as they are passed. This is called coprophagy, and it is a normal part of hamster digestion. The hamster is able to absorb the vitamins and nutrients contained in the pellets the second time they pass through the small intestine. If a hamster is unable to do this, due to paralyis or an injury, it may become deficient in essential vitamins.

The colon, which is long in hamsters, is important for the absorption of water and electrolytes (salts). Once these have been extracted, only waste products are left, which are formed into hard, dark faeces. These travel through the rectum, which connects the colon and the anus (bottom), and are expelled from the anus. The faeces are much harder than the soft pellets formed by the caecum, so they do not trigger an eating response in the hamster.

4. ENDOCRINE SYSTEM

The endocrine system consists of numerous endocrine glands. These ductless glands are situated throughout the body, producing chemical messengers (hormones) that are secreted into the bloodstream, affecting different areas of the body. The hormones regulate the internal environment and metabolism of the body, influencing behaviour and activity.

The thyroid, parathyroid, adrenal, and pituitary glands are all examples of endocrine glands. Some organs, such as ovaries, testes and the pancreas, also have endocrine tissue among their other cells.

THYROID GLAND

This consists of two lobes, one either side of the trachea (windpipe), just below the larynx (voice box). In cold conditions the thyroid gland releases more of its hormone, which increases the body's metabolic rate. Low levels of the hormone, as occurs in hypothyroidism, result in lethargy and weight gain. Thyroid hormone is also needed for growth and reproduction.

PARATHYROID GLANDS

These are two small glands situated next to the thyroid. They produce a hormone that regulates calcium levels in the blood.

ADRENAL GLANDS

These are small glands found in the abdomen, just in front of the kidneys. Males possess larger glands than females, which is the opposite of most other rodent species.

The adrenal glands produce four main types of hormone:

- **Cortisol:** A steroid that, among other things, affects blood glucose and protein metabolism. An excess of cortisol is responsible for the symptoms of Cushing's disease (see page 90).
- **Aldosterone:** This influences the kidneys, to maintain the salt balance in the body.
- **Sex hormones:** In males, the adrenal glands produce androgens, while in females, oestrogens are produced.
- **Adrenaline and Noradrenaline:** These are hormones that are produced under stress and prepare the body for fight or flight.

PITUITARY GLAND

The pituitary gland is situated at the base of the brain. It produces hormones to stimulate the adrenal, thyroid, and sex glands. It also produces a growth hormone, prolactin (stimulates milk production), oxytocin (helps with birth and milk production), and vasopressin (controls water resorption in the kidneys). Most of these hormones are controlled by a system called negative feedback. When a hormone is released, it triggers the release of another substance. When that second substance reaches too high a level, it causes a reduction in the original hormone.

5. URINARY SYSTEM

Urine is a watery fluid containing the body's waste products and some poisons. The water concentration of the urine is regulated, to help control the fluid balance in the body. The urinary system is responsible for removing urine from the body. The system consists of an upper (producing) and a lower (storage) part. The upper part includes the kidneys (where urine is produced) and the ureters (tubes to transport the urine to the lower part). The lower part includes the bladder (where urine is stored) and the urethra (the exit tube from the body).

Hamsters have two kidneys, situated in the abdomen just below, and either side of, the backbone. The right kidney is further forward than the left one. Blood enters the kidneys via the renal arteries, which come straight from the aorta, the main artery of the body. Inside the kidneys there are structures called glomeruli. When urine enters the kidneys it is filtered through the glomeruli. Large proteins are prevented from leaving the bloodstream, but smaller particles, containing waste products, are filtered out of the blood. The fluid passing through is further altered in the kidney tubules before being formed into urine. The kidney tubules are long passages that reabsorb salts and plasma back into the bloodstream. Hormones also influence the tubules, altering the amount of water reabsorbed. For example, in a dehydrated animal, more water is reabsorbed, so that the final urine produced is highly concentrated and small in volume.

The tubules empty urine into a central collection area in the kidney. From there, urine travels along the thin, muscular tubes of the ureters to the bladder. Muscular contractions in the ureters ensure urine passes in one direction only, i.e. towards the bladder.

The bladder is the storage vessel for urine. It expands considerably when full and shrinks when empty. The strong muscle in the wall of the bladder prevents urine leaking out in a healthy individual. When the bladder becomes full, and the hamster urinates, urine exits the body by the urethra – a single muscular tube that exits the body at the tip of the penis in males, and just below the vagina in females.

URINARY SYSTEM PROBLEMS

A healthy Syrian hamster weighing approximately 4.2 ounces (120 grammes) produces about 7 ml of urine per day. Other species of hamsters should produce an equivalent volume in relation to weight. The pH level in urine from a healthy hamster is usually slightly alkaline (about 8). Normal urine is thick, yellow, and contains small crystals that make it appear turbid and milky. This should not be confused with pus or infection. However, the crystals can become a problem if they join together to form stones (see Urolithiasis, page 108).

If the filtering mechanism in the kidneys becomes damaged, larger protein molecules are lost from the blood and pass out in the urine. These show up as protein on a urine dipstick test, although a low level of protein may be normal in hamster urine. If protein continues to be lost, the hamster will slowly lose weight, particularly muscle. Unfortunately, many hamsters produce the abnormal protein amyloid, which can damage the filtering mechanism in the glomeruli.

If the kidney tubules are damaged, they lose the ability to concentrate urine. Consequently, lots of watery urine is produced and the hamster drinks more to compensate for this constant loss of fluid. This type of damage is usually caused by the waste products and poisons being excreted from the body. Certain drugs, such as some antibiotics and painkillers, are particularly damaging to kidney tubules.

Kidneys are normally very efficient and resilient – a hamster with less than 50 per cent kidney function may still appear perfectly healthy. However, the kidneys cannot adapt to stresses such as heat, dehydration, or diarrhoea, as they are unable to retain enough fluid. Signs of kidney failure may become apparent after stresses such as heat stroke, which also causes further damage from dehydration.

6. REPRODUCTIVE SYSTEM

Hamsters become sexually mature from approximately 30 to 40 days after birth. Breeding generally begins from 6 to 10 weeks of age in females, and 10 to 14 in males, although many breeders choose to delay the first litter in their captive-bred hamsters for health reasons (see section three).

FEMALE

The female reproductive organs are internal and external. The internal parts include the mammary glands, the ovaries, the uterus and the vagina. The external parts include the nipples of the mammary glands and the vulva (the entrance to the vagina).

A female hamster has two mammary glands that run along the outside of the abdomen wall. The mammary glands produce milk when the hamster has young to feed. The milk is produced from six or seven pairs of evenly spaced nipples, which are visible on the hamster's chest.

Female Reproductive System

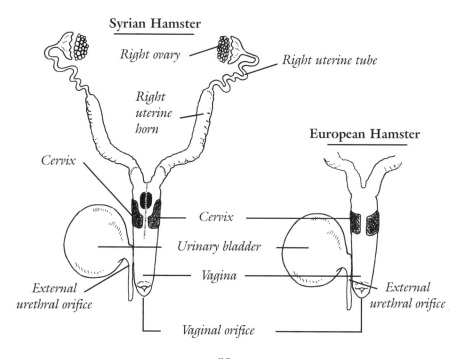

80

The two ovaries, which are situated in the fat behind the kidneys, produce female hormones and follicles. Follicles are fluid-filled structures that grow inside the ovaries to nourish the unfertilised ova (eggs) contained in the ovaries. When the follicles rupture, ova are propelled down a long coiled tube, called the oviduct or fallopian tube, to the uterus. This is termed ovulation. Oestrus is the time around ovulation, when a female comes into season and is ready to breed.

The uterus has two sides, called horns. Externally, these horns appear to be joined, but in the Syrian hamster they are separated internally. Each horn has a separate cervix, and both cervixes open side by side into the vagina.

Like most rodents, the vagina is exclusive to the reproductive tract and is not linked to any other bodily function. The opening of the vagina – the vulva – is situated below the anus (bottom). The urethra (passage from the bladder) opens separately, just below the vulva.

OESTRUS AND PREGNANCY

Females cycle every four days (except in winter), with oestrus lasting for a few hours. When a female hamster approaches oestrus, she produces a thin, translucent mucus from her vulva. Once ovulation has passed, the mucus becomes white, opaque, and slightly sticky. This thicker discharge means oestrus has passed, and, if the hamster is to conceive, mating must be tried three days later, in the evening.

After mating, a thick vaginal plug forms, to keep the ova and sperm inside the uterus. Fertilised eggs implant into the uterus after six days, and pregnancy lasts between 15 and 16 days. If the female fails to conceive, she should produce the discharges associated with oestrus five and nine days after the unsuccessful mating attempt. If these discharges are absent, this normally means that the female is pregnant.

A pregnant female will gain weight rapidly, and will develop a swollen abdomen approximately 10 days into her pregnancy. At this time, the young may be felt inside her body, by placing a finger and thumb either side of the abdomen and squeezing with the gentlest of pressure. However, some of the smaller breeds can show surprisingly few signs of pregnancy – the first indication being the squeaking of newborn hamsters in the cage!

The female comes into oestrus soon after giving birth, although this is usually infertile. A fertile oestrus cycle will normally occur between 2 and 18 days after weaning, which is when young are approximately 21 days old.

MALE

Male hamsters have two prominent testicles, contained in a scrotal sac situated between and behind the rear legs. This makes the rear end of a mature male look quite rounded when viewed from above, particularly when compared to the more pointed profile of a female. Males have a greater distance from the anus to the penis than the distance from the anus to vaginal opening in females, and this feature can be used to tell the sex of young hamsters before the testicles are obvious.

When a male hamster is born, his testicles are held inside the abdomen. After birth, the testicles descend to the scrotal sac through the inguinal canal in the groin area. This canal stays open throughout life, so, unlike many species, hamsters can withdraw their testicles back into their body. This often happens when a hamster becomes cold.

Male Reproductive System

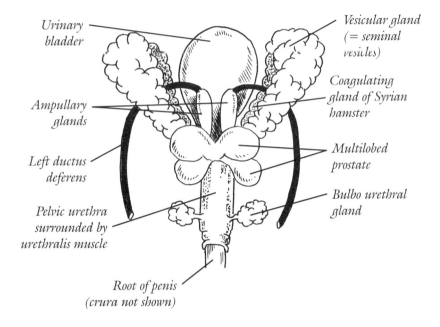

Urinary bladder

Vesicular gland (= seminal vesicles)

Ampullary glands

Coagulating gland of Syrian hamster

Left ductus deferens

Multilobed prostate

Pelvic urethra surrounded by urethralis muscle

Bulbo urethral gland

Root of penis (crura not shown)

The main body of the testicle is called the testis, which produces sperm. Sperm is stored in the epididymis – a coiled, tube-like structure attached to the testis – until it becomes mature and is ejaculated. The testes also produce the male hormone testosterone, which is responsible for the sexual, and sometimes aggressive, behaviour of a mature male.

When a male hamster mates with a female, sperm passes out of the epididymis and travels along the spermatic cord (in the ductus deferens) to the urethra. Here it is mixed with nutritional fluid from the accessory sex glands, to form semen. The accessory sex glands include the seminal vesicles, the prostate gland (found near the bladder), and the bulbo urethral gland. Semen is ejaculated from the urethra at the end of the penis. The penis of a hamster points backwards from the body, underneath the anus. It contains a small bone called the os penis.

CHAPTER 9

A-Z OF HAMSTER DISEASES AND HEALTH PROBLEMS

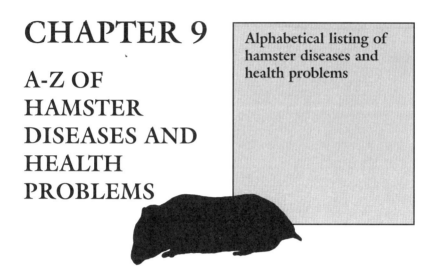

Alphabetical listing of hamster diseases and health problems

A

ABSCESS

A localised collection of pus.

Signs: Abscesses can appear anywhere on the body. They are swellings that can be soft and non-painful, or hard and sore if pressure builds up from the amount of pus contained in them. Chronic or long-standing abscesses are surrounded by a thickened capsule of fibrous tissue, which makes them feel hard to the touch, although they are not usually painful. There may be a discharge, making the coat damp and matted. Abscesses can feel similar to tumours, so further investigation may be necessary. Abscesses on the face or jaw are often related to teeth problems, while internal abscesses can cause a variety of symptoms (such as anorexia, abdominal pain and respiratory problems), depending on where they are situated.

Cause: Abscesses are caused by bacterial infection entering through a wound, such as a bite or a cut, or in the mouth from a rotten tooth root. Internal abscesses are caused by bacteria spreading in the bloodstream, often following a respiratory infection. The most common bacteria at fault include *Staphylococcus aureus, Pasteurella pneumotropica* and *Streptococcus species*. Many healthy hamsters carry small amounts of these, but the bacteria multiply to form pus in sites of damage.

Treatment: Abscesses on the body should be lanced and cleaned with salt water or a disinfectant. Large or multiple abscesses may also need a course of antibiotics. Tooth root abscesses can be more difficult to clear, as they usually require a course of antibiotics and removal of the affected tooth, which is a delicate operation under general anaesthetic.

ACARIASIS
A skin disorder cause by the *Demodex* mite.
Signs: Hair loss combined with dry, scaly skin and some spots. The head and neck are particularly affected. This is not usually pruritic (itchy).
Cause: There are two species of demodex mite that infect hamsters, *Demodex aurati* and *Demodex criceti*. These live deep in the hair root on many hamsters without causing problems. However, animals with a weakened immune system, such as young, pregnant or geriatric hamsters, or those unwell for another reason, may develop an allergic reaction. The mites cannot be seen with the naked eye and can be difficult to find on skin scrapings. You may need to make several visits to your vet.
Treatment: A drug called Ivermectin is highly effective, and may be used to treat *Sarcoptic Mange* as well. Weekly bathing in a drug called Amritraz is also effective, but bathing hamsters can be very stressful to hamster and owner alike.

AGGRESSION
Aggression is a normal part of hamster behaviour, but it can become problematic when it is directed towards owners, particularly children.
Signs: Biting or sitting on haunches making a squeaking noise.
Cause: Hamsters are short-sighted and nocturnal. They are easily startled by unexpected movements, being awakened suddenly, or by being picked up, and they may resort to a natural defence of attack. Deafness will make them unaware of approach and more likely to bite in fear. Syrian hamsters are naturally aggressive towards each other, and should be housed separately. Most hamsters become more aggressive when they are unwell.
Treatment: Hamsters (like many people) are bad-tempered when disturbed from sleep, so they should be handled during active periods in the evening or early morning. Most will become used to regular and gentle handling.

ALLERGY
An exaggerated reaction (such as sneezing, itching, and skin rashes) to a substance that has no effect on most individuals.
Signs: Sneezing, ocular (eye) discharge, dermatitis and swollen feet are the most common symptoms. Discharges from the eyes and nose are normally clear, but may become thicker and pus-like if there is a secondary infection.
Cause: The most common substances causing allergic reactions (known as allergens) are food and bedding, particularly if dusty. Smoke (from cigarettes or fire), aerosol sprays, and even perfume can also cause allergic reaction. Some allergies may be hereditary.
Treatment: Finding the cause of the allergy is the most important measure. Bedding should be changed (preferably to the shredded-paper or non-dusty hay variety) and all sawdust or synthetic material should be removed from the cage. Coloured paper must never be used, because printing inks are toxic to hamsters. Dietary allergies may be caused by sunflower seeds, peanuts, or coloured biscuits (which contain dyes

and E numbers). These can be replaced with cooked rice, fruit, and porridge made with water not milk. It may take a week or more for the symptoms to lessen. Meanwhile, the eyes and nose should be kept clean with water or saline. Severe cases may need steroid drops or cream.

ALOPECIA
Loss of hair.
Signs: Localised areas of hair loss, or general hair loss all over the body. Hair loss may be accompanied by pruritis (itching).
Cause: A number of skin infections and parasites can be the cause *(see Ringworm, Demodex, and Sarcoptic Mange)*. Hair loss may also be a symptom of disease *(see Cushing's Disease, Hypothyroidism, and Kidney Disease)*. Diets containing less than 16 per cent protein, or excess cereals, can cause alopecia. It frequently occurs in geriatric hamsters as part of the ageing process, beginning with two bald patches developing on either side of the backbone.
Treatment: Skin infections or underlying diseases need special treatment. The protein level of the diet should be checked and amended if necessary. Feeding more fruit and vegetables can help to overcome the negative effects of too much cereal. One or two drops of cod liver oil and a yeast tablet added to the daily food allowance can also improve symptoms. Cod liver oil needs to be given for several weeks before much improvement is noticeable. Giving more will not speed the process and may cause diarrhoea.

AMPUTATION
The surgical removal of a limb or part of a limb. This may be necessary after a severe break or infection in the bone. Most hamsters manage remarkably well on three legs, although they will need nursing and pain relief (e.g. aspirin) for a few days following surgery.

AMYLOIDOSIS
An abnormal type of protein that accumulates in various organs.
Signs: Symptoms are more common in females than in males, and vary according to which organs are affected and how badly. Amyloidosis is a common cause of kidney failure and also damages the liver, heart and adrenal glands. Kidney damage may result in severe leaking of protein into the urine, with resultant fluid loss and ascites (i.e. fluid pooling in the abdomen). This is known as nephrotic syndrome; a similar condition occurs in other species, particularly certain breeds of dog.
Cause: Excess production of the hormone amyloid (amyloidosis) is thought to be the result of an abnormal immune response. It is more common in some family lines.
Treatment: There is no cure or treatment to prevent the release of the hormone amyloid, although the symptoms can be given supportive treatment *(see Kidney Disease, Liver Disease, and Heart Disease)*.

ANOREXIA
Loss of appetite.
Signs: Eating little or nothing. If this is due to tooth problems the hamster may have a wet chin from dribbling.

Cause: Anorexia is often caused by problems with the teeth *(see Malocclusion)* or mouth *(see Impacted Cheek Pouches)*. Foreign bodies obstructing the mouth may also prevent the hamster from eating. Other common causes include an obstruction or impaction in the digestive tract *(see Impaction)*, or any general illness (most animals, including humans, lose their appetite when unwell). Older hamsters suffering from kidney failure can develop anorexia but other symptoms are usually noticeable before failure to eat.

Treatment: Prompt veterinary attention is needed. Once the underlying cause has been treated, the hamster should be given plenty of fluids and tempted to eat with any favourite foods. Fluids may be given by mouth, or, in serious illness, a veterinary surgeon will inject some under the skin or directly into the abdomen (known as intra peritoneally). Porridge is palatable to most hamsters and can be syringe-fed if needed. After suffering from any digestive problems, hamsters should be given probiotics – a mix of the bacteria that aid digestion, which usually live in the stomach and intestines. There are suitable varieties marketed for dogs and cats, which may be prescribed in appropriate dosages for hamsters.

B

BALDNESS
See Alopecia, and Satinisation.

BEHAVIOURAL PROBLEMS
See Aggression, and Cannibalism.

BLADDER PROBLEMS
See Cystitis, Urolithiasis, and Haematuria.

BLINDNESS
Loss of sight.
Signs: When a hamster goes blind gradually, it adapts very well. Indeed, you may not notice your hamster is blind if it is kept in the same cage, with the same cage furnishings situated in the same place. However, a blind hamster will bump into new objects placed in the cage, or will crash into items when it is allowed out of its cage. Some causes of blindness may make the eye look abnormal *(see Cataracts)*.

Cause: Some hamsters are born without eyes, due to a genetic condition (see page 142. Blindness can also be caused by progression of disease *(see Diabetes, and Glaucoma)*. Geriatric hamsters may go blind due to the ageing process, in which case the lens will look cloudy, but not as opaque as a cataract. Hamsters may go blind in one or both eyes after a stroke, although this is not necessarily permanent.

Treatment: Hamsters that have suffered a stroke may recover sight within a few days or weeks. There is no treatment for the other causes. Climbing apparatus and ledges should be removed from the cage to prevent the hamster from falling. Exercise outside the cage should be stopped or closely supervised.

BRONCHITIS
See Respiratory Disease.

C

CAGE PARALYSIS
Loss of use of the hind legs. Not be confused with *Hind Limb Paralysis*.
Signs: The hamster will lose the use of its hind legs, which will be dragged stiffly behind it. Severely affected hamsters may be completely unable to move.
Cause: Probably caused by a lack of exercise exacerbated by a diet low in vitamins, particularly vitamins D and E.
Treatment: Cases caught early enough will recover if the hamster is encouraged to take a little exercise every day and given a vitamin supplement. Once recovered, the hamster should be encouraged to exercise by providing a wheel, climbing apparatus, and allowing time to roam out of the cage. Obese individuals should have their food quantity reduced, particularly tidbits and sunflower seeds. Late-diagnosed cases may not recover fully.

CANCER
The term for malignant growths *(see Tumours)*.

CANNIBALISM
When an animal eats its own kind.
Signs: Cannibalism usually takes the form of a female hamster eating her own young.
Cause: Common causes include the provision of insufficient nesting material, disturbing the nest or the nursing mother, and inadequate diet. It is more common among females that have just had their first litter or a particularly large litter.
Treatment: Sufficient bedding material should be provided for the female to make a good nest in advance of the birth. The protein level of the diet can be increased by adding a little hard-boiled egg, cheese, or powdered baby milk. The cage should be placed somewhere warm and quiet and left undisturbed for several days.

CARIES
A type of tooth decay, similar to that seen in humans, which weakens the teeth and makes them susceptible to breakage or infection.
Signs: Anorexia or dribbling, with possible facial swelling if an abscess develops in the tooth root.
Cause: Caries are most common among hamsters fed a diet high in starch or acids, particularly when they include treats and snacks intended for humans. Genetic susceptibility may also play a part, as is probably the case in humans.
Treatment: A prolonged course of antibiotics may be needed if the tooth has become infected. Extraction may be the best course of action for badly affected teeth, but this can be a very difficult procedure. The lack of surgical instruments suitable for use on such small teeth, and the difficulty in gaining access to the back of a hamster's mouth, make extraction unsuitable in some cases. Gags and cheek expanders, designed for rabbits and guinea pigs, are too large for hamsters.

CASTRATION
Surgical removal of a male's testicles, commonly carried out to remove cancerous growths. Although anaesthesia carries a risk in all rodents, modern anaesthetics and increased veterinary knowledge has led to more surgery being

carried out in hamsters. Many vets now recommend surgery and find it an interesting challenge.

CATARACTS
An opacity in the lens of the eye making it appear light blue or white. Advanced cataracts cause blindness. Cataracts may be congenital or age-related, and are often caused by *Diabetes*.

COLLAPSE
A state of immobility.
Signs: The hamster may collapse during exercise, or may be found in a semi-conscious state.
Cause: The most likely cause during exercise is *Heart Disease*. Prolonged collapse (where the hamster is alive but not improving) is likely to be due to extremes of temperature *(see Hibernation, and Heat Stroke)*. Pregnant females may collapse as the result of a calcium deficiency *(see Eclampsia)*. Any severe disease will cause collapse before death.
Treatment: After determining the cause and providing any specific treatment, the patient should be kept quiet, in a constant temperature, and given plenty of fluids. A tiny drop of brandy may also help.

CONJUNCTIVITIS
An inflammation of the conjunctiva (the skin inside the eyelids).
Signs: Discharge from the eyes. The eyes may appear reddened and sore, and may be partially closed.
Cause: Can be caught as an infection from other hamsters, or caused through irritation from dust and fumes, etc. Irritation may cause conjunctivitis without infection, and it is often a sign of an *Allergy*.
Treatment: The cage should be removed from draughts or any dusty or smoky environment. Eye drops or cream will help to soothe the irritation. If there is an infection, the drops will need to contain antibiotics.

CONSTIPATION AND IMPACTION
Impaction is an extreme form of constipation, where there is a total obstruction of the gut with dry material.
Signs: The hamster will appear miserable, sitting hunched over with an arched back. The abdomen will be swollen, turning a deep-pink or purple colour in time. The anus will be very prominent, due to straining, and may also be red and swollen. Few or no droppings will be passed and the hamster may be seen straining.
Cause: An inadequate water supply causes hard dry droppings and subsequent constipation. Hamsters are particularly susceptible during weaning. Baby hamsters that are not accustomed to using a water bottle, or experience difficulty reaching the spout, may become dehydrated. This, combined with the drier and more solid food given during weaning, can lead to dehydration, which can develop into constipation or impaction. Impaction may also be caused if the hamster eats cotton wool (cotton) or synthetically produced bedding. Escaped hamsters will often eat bits of fibre such as curtains, which causes the same effect. Lack of exercise makes individuals more susceptible, especially if associated with overfeeding and *Obesity*. An infestation of

internal parasites can also cause impaction, although this is rare *(see Worms)*.

Treatment: Laxatives need to be given in small quantities – an overdose can lead to further problems *(see Intususseption, and Rectal Prolapse)*. One or two drops of liquid paraffin, olive oil, or lactulose should be given by mouth, three times daily, until faeces are passed.

Laxative plants (e.g. dandelion leaves or lettuce) should be offered and continued in small amounts for a few days after the obstruction has passed. The provision of plenty of fluids is essential, to lubricate the faeces and to prevent dehydration and the possible death of the patient. If the hamster will not drink, fluids can be given orally, using a dropper or small syringe. However, if the hamster cannot swallow freely, fluids must be injected directly under the skin, a procedure that should be done by a vet.

To prevent further episodes, all artificial bedding should be discarded, and there must be easy access to a constant supply of clean fresh water. Adding some green food to the daily diet will also help.

COPROPHAGY
When an animal eats its own faeces.
This is a normal process in hamsters (see page 77). Problems may arise when a hamster is unable to do this due to physical disabilities *(see Hind Leg Paralysis)* or teeth problems *(see Malocclusion)*. Inability to eat the faeces can lead to digestive problems and vitamin deficiencies.

CORNEAL ULCER
A damaged area in the cornea of the eye.
Signs: Corneal ulcers are painful, so the hamster is likely to keep the affected eye partially closed. There may also be a discharge, which may be clear or infected. It is sometimes possible to see the defect on the surface of the eye, which may appear slightly cloudy or 'blue' due to the swelling.

Cause: Anything coming into contact with the cornea may scratch it, the most common culprits being straw or hay seeds. *Entropion* will also cause ulceration, and usually affects both eyes.

Treatment: Antibiotic eye drops are usually prescribed, and will need to be administered three or four times daily. The size of the ulcer can be seen with a dye called fluorescin, which attaches itself to the damaged cornea, making it bright green. This is repeated after a few days to check that the ulcer is healing and decreasing in size. Severe ulceration can cause the eye to burst, in which case removal will be necessary.

CRYPTORCHIDISM
An uncommon condition when one or both testicles do not descend into the scrotal sac.
Hamsters have the ability to withdraw their testicles back inside the body, and may do so under certain circumstances, but if the testicles are never visible in the scrotal sac, the hamster is cryptorchid.

Hamsters with this condition are often infertile or sub-fertile. Cryptorchidism is believed to be a heritable trait, so affected hamsters should not be used for breeding.

CUSHING'S DISEASE
A disease caused by overproduction of cortisol from the adrenal glands *(see Hyperadrenocorticism).*

Signs: The most common sign is *Alopecia,* usually accompanied by an increase in pigment of the skin. *Obesity, Polydipsia and Polyuria,* and abdominal enlargement may also be seen.

Cause: Cushing's Disease is normally caused by primary disease in the glands, such as a tumour, or a secondary complaint in the pituitary gland (part of the brain). The pituitary gland produces ACTH hormone, which regulates the adrenal glands. Disease in the pituitary gland is also due to a tumour in most cases.

Treatment: Low doses of drugs used for treating the canine version of the disorder have been used with some success. Tablets are divided up and dissolved in syrup, to be given by mouth.

CYSTITIS
Inflammation of the bladder.

Signs: There is usually blood in the urine *(see Haematuria)* and the hamster may seem uncomfortable, particularly when trying to pass urine. The urine is thicker than normal and may be smelly. The smell, combined with an increased need to clean the cage, may be the first signs noted.

Cause: Cystitis is usually caused by a bacterial infection and may be associated with *Urolithiasis* or *Kidney Disease*.

Treatment: Antibiotics are given by injection or in the drinking water or feed. If a urine sample can be obtained, a laboratory investigation will grow the bacteria and find the best antibiotics to treat the infection. Fluids are important to flush the bladder. Often, the hamster will be drinking more anyway, and electrolytes can be added to the water bottle to prevent dehydration. If the hamster does not appear to be drinking sufficiently, extra fluids should be given by dropper. Feeding fresh greens may also help.

If cystitis does not disappear, or if it recurs, further investigation will be needed to find and treat the underlying cause.

D

DEAFNESS
An inability to hear.

Signs: Failure to respond to noise. Deaf hamsters may be more aggressive to people and other hamsters – they cannot hear anything approaching and so react with more fear *(see Aggression)*.

Cause: Deafness may be temporary, caused by an infection or a physical obstruction in the ear, such as a discharge, a foreign body, or excess wax *(see Ear Mites)*. Permanent deafness can be due to changes in the inner ear after a stroke, as part of the ageing process, or as an adverse reaction to the antibiotic Streptomycin. Streptomycin is rarely used in modern veterinary medicine to treat hamsters due to other toxic side effects.

Treatment: Unless caused by ear mites or infections, there is no treatment. Deaf hamsters should be approached slowly, with caution, so they can see the handler's hand before they are touched.

DEMODEX
Mites that live on the skin of many healthy hamsters but can cause skin problems in others *(see Acariasis).*

DIABETES
A common condition among elderly hamsters, in which insufficient levels of insulin are produced.
Signs: The main symptoms are an increase in thirst and urination *(see Polydipsia and Polyuria)*, which may be accompanied by gradual weight loss and the development of cataracts. Individuals are also more susceptible to urine infections, due to increased glucose in the urine, which encourages bacterial growth *(see Cystitis)*. A simple dipstick test on a few drops of urine will check for glucose.
Cause: Either a lack of insulin produced by the pancreas, or failure of the body to respond to insulin. Insulin is a hormone that regulates the passing of glucose from blood into cells. Cells need glucose for energy, in order to function. The extra glucose is excreted in the urine, drawing more water with it, which leads to dehydration. The symptom of increased thirst is the body's way of attempting to replace the fluid loss. The disease is more common among Russian and Chinese hamsters, and is probably inherited.
Treatment: It is important to avoid stress, as this makes the disease worse. Even moving the cage to a new area or room can trigger symptoms. There must always be plenty of fresh water present, and the cage should be cleaned more often, due to increased urine production. Adding fibre (e.g. high-fibre breakfast cereals) to the diet may help to regulate blood glucose. Individuals suffering from diabetes can live for some time, but they should not be bred from – females will become worse during pregnancy, and the disease is hereditary in many cases.

DIARRHOEA
Loose or watery faeces. Diarrhoea is common among pet hamsters, and may be a symptom of a more serious, underlying disease. It should always be treated promptly as the resulting dehydration can be fatal.
Signs: Frequent loose or watery faeces. The rear end may be soiled and damp *(see Wet Tail)*. Infectious causes of diarrhoea result in severe illness, with the hamster hunched over in an uncomfortable position, refusing to eat *(see Anorexia)*, and reluctant to move. In less severe cases, there will be noticeable weight loss and an increased thirst. If diarrhoea is caused by dietary problems, the hamster will normally continue to eat and should appear bright and healthy initially.
Cause: Infectious causes include *Wet Tail*, *Tyzzer's Disease*, *Salmonella*, and *Yersinia*. Any sudden change in diet, wet green food, food straight from the refrigerator, and overfeeding laxative plants (e.g. dandelion or groundsel) can cause diarrhoea. Some antibiotics may induce diarrhoea by killing the 'helpful' bacteria in the gut, which allows more harmful bugs to multiply and produce endotoxins that damage the intestines.
Treatment: Veterinary attention should be sought promptly. Antibiotics are prescribed if a specific disease is diagnosed or suspected, although accurate diagnosis usually requires samples to be sent to a laboratory. It is vital that plenty of fluids are given, to counteract dehydration. In serious cases, oral rehydration fluids should be given by dropper every hour, and the patient should be kept warm and clean, in

strict isolation. Initially, up to 3 mls of intravenous drip fluid may be given by injection under the skin. Food should be withheld for 24 hours. In addition, two to three drops of kaolin preparations or charcoal can be given by mouth three times a day. The diet should be checked and no green foods given until two to three days after full recovery. Probiotics are useful when antibiotics have been prescribed; several proprietary brands licensed for use in dogs and cats are suitable.

DISLOCATION
Displacement of a bone from its normal position in relation to a joint. Hips and hocks are the most likely places.
Signs: Sudden lameness. The affected leg looks abnormal, and may appear to bend the 'wrong' way at the affected joint.
Cause: Usually an accident, such as falling or getting a leg stuck in the exercise wheel.
Treatment: Dislocated bones cause damage to the surrounding ligaments and tendons that support the joint. Therefore, the bone should be replaced, and support should be given to the leg while the ligaments heal. It is difficult to apply dressings to a hamster's leg, and many hamsters frequently chew the dressings. Sellotape can provide a solution, as it is rigid but lightweight. Dislocated bones may require a general anaesthetic to reset them, and painkillers should be given for a few days. In cases where it is impossible to replace the bone, or if it recurs, it may be necessary to remove the affected bone *(see Amputation)*.

DYSTOCIA
Difficulty during birth.
Signs: The hamster will be restless. She will have prepared her nest but, as yet, produced no young. She may have a bloody discharge.
Cause: Oversized young or *Eclampsia* will prevent parturition (birth). There may be no obvious cause.
Treatment: Small amounts of oxytocin and calcium injections should induce birth. A little honey and water by mouth will give the female extra energy. If this is unsuccessful, a Caesarean section should be performed. The young are unlikely to survive, but surgery may save the female's life, although she is unlikely to breed again.

E

EAR MITES
Tiny insects that live in the ear.
Signs: The ears will be full of dark-coloured wax, and there will be crusty spots on the ears, face, feet and genitals (caused by rubbing the ears). Males suffer spots on the face, feet and genitals more than females. Irritation of the ears will cause the hamster to shake its head.
Cause: The hamster ear mite is called *Notoedres notoedres*. Hamsters can also be infected by the feline ear mite *Notoedres cati*. This is surprising, as they must come in close contact to a cat's ear or face to contract the mite! Mites are normally caught from another hamster, often the mother, and may be present for some time before symptoms are manifested.
Treatment: The cattle and sheep wormer Ivermectin is the best treatment. It should

be diluted and given as a tiny injection or as a drop in the mouth. A second treatment will be needed after 10 days, and more than two treatments may be necessary.

ECLAMPSIA
A disease of the final stage of pregnancy or soon after whelping.
Signs: Collapse and an inability to move, which may progress to convulsions (*see Fits*) and death. In late pregnancy, whelping will stop.
Cause: Insufficient calcium in the blood. This may be due to an increased need for calcium (if the female is carrying a large litter or if she is lactating) or an insufficient supply from a poor diet, particularly if the food contains a lot of sunflower seeds, which are low in calcium.
Treatment: This is an emergency situation requiring prompt veterinary attention. Calcium is injected under the skin so that it can take effect immediately. The diet should be corrected, and, until the babies are weaned, calcium supplements should be given – palatable dog tablets can be crushed and sprinkled on the hamster's food.

ECZEMA
A term for scaly and itchy conditions of the skin *(see Scurf)*.

ENTROPION
An inwardly turned eyelid that rubs the surface of the eye.
Signs: One or both eyes may be affected. The eye will appear sore, partly closed, and there may be some discharge. On closer examination it can be seen that the eyelid is turned in, touching the surface of the eye.
Cause: This is usually a congenital problem (i.e. the hamster is affected from birth), particularly in rex-coated and Dwarf hamsters. Another cause is *Weight Loss*, as, when fatty deposits behind the eye are lost, the eye sinks further back in the socket, pulling in the eyelids. This is more likely in older hamsters.
Treatment: In mild cases, administering eye cream to ease the irritation, and pulling the skin with a finger, to evert the eyelid, can be successful. However, this must be repeated for many days. More severe cases need surgery, or an injection under the eyelid to push it out, both of these treatments being carried out under a general anaesthetic. Hamsters born with entropion should not be bred from, as the condition is inherited.

EVERTED CHEEK POUCHES
The cheek pouches are not fixed in place and can become turned inside out.
They can usually be reverted quite easily, although a short general anaesthetic may be required for lively patients.

EYE PROLAPSE
The whole eye may fall from the socket or the contents of the eye may burst out through a ruptured cornea (the surface of the eye).
Signs: The eye is hanging out and there may be blood or a discharge. The eye rapidly dries and shrinks.
Cause: Trauma is the most likely cause, particularly fighting injuries.
Treatment: Enucleation (surgical removal) is relatively straightforward.

F

FALSE PREGNANCY
See Pseudopregnancy.

FIRST AID
Most households will contain medicines that are suitable for use on hamsters in an emergency. Shocked or injured hamsters should be kept warm and quiet. Any ill hamster will benefit from fluids. If electrolytes designed for dogs and cats are available, they are suitable, otherwise water will suffice. Aspirin can be used as a painkiller, at a dose of 10 mg per 100 grammes. Vapour rub is useful for chest infections, and brandy has revived many a comatose hamster!

FITS
Fits (also known as convulsions or seizures) are more likely in older hamsters, usually as a symptom of another, underlying disease.
Signs: A series of convulsions, during which the hamster has no control over its body.
Cause: Epilepsy is rare in hamsters, and fits are usually a sign of some other disease, such as *Hamster Plague, Diabetes, Liver Disease, Eclampsia,* or head trauma. *Lymphocytic Choriomeningitis Virus (LCMV)* is another cause. It is not thought to be present in the UK, but should always be considered because it poses a risk to humans.
Treatment: Fits are alarming to watch but rarely last long. The hamster should be kept in a dark, quiet environment to recover, and the cause should be investigated.

FLEAS
Hamsters can be infested with fleas from dogs or cats in the same household. No direct contact between the dog or cat and the hamster is necessary.
Signs: Pruritis (itching) with scurfy skin. Fleas are visible to the naked eye and can be seen by parting the coat. They are brown and move quickly. Another sign is flea dirt – black specks, deep in the coat, which turn red when a drop of water is added (flea dirt is mainly dried blood). This is easier to see if the dirt is placed on white paper first.
Treatment: Pyrethrin powder or spray, such as bird anti-mite spray, should be applied sparingly and repeated after one week. Alternatively, your vet can provide you with some Fipronil (the basis of some commerical sprays and spot-on treatments), which is also effective. Fipronil should be used at a low dose, covering a quarter to a third of the body every few days to avoid overdose. All household pets should be treated, to avoid reinfection, although veterinary advice must be sought before treating rabbits.
   Cages should be cleaned out, bedding destroyed, and the cage sprayed with anti-mite spray.

FOOT AND MOUTH DISEASE
Hamsters are susceptible to this contagious viral disease of domestic livestock. As they are generally kept separately inside the house, hamsters are not culled on infected farms. However, an escaping hamster could be at risk.

FRACTURES
Hamsters have small leg bones in proportion to their overall body size, and leg fractures are common. Fractures of the spine or ribs are rare.
Signs: Sudden lameness. The affected leg may swing loosely or be held at an unusual angle.
Cause: Generally due to an accident *(see Dislocation)*. A calcium deficiency, caused by a diet high in sunflower seeds, for example, will cause weakening of the bones and make them more susceptible to fracture.
Treatment: The fractured bone will need to be supported until it is healed. It is possible to perform internal fixation, by pinning a bone with thin wire, although few veterinary surgeons have attempted this. Until the bone has healed, the hamster should be kept in a tank with nothing to climb and no wheel to exercise in. Healing is normally very rapid, with new bone laid down around the fracture within ten days. *Amputation* may be needed for severe or non-healing fractures.

G

GLAUCOMA
A condition in which pressure in the eyeball is much greater than normal.
Signs: Swelling of the eye globe. The hamster may show signs of distress, as the condition is painful in the early stages.
Cause: Glaucoma can be a result of injury impairing normal eye drainage. It is also an inherited condition in Campbell hamsters.
Treatment: Eye cream is applied to the bulging surface of the eye to prevent trauma. If the eye ruptures, or if it is very painful, it should be removed. Hamsters with inherited Glaucoma should not be bred from.

H

HAEMATURIA
Blood in the urine.
Signs: Blood in the urine. The blood may be fresh and obvious, or the urine may be stained a dark brown-red colour. Depending on the cause, the hamster may also appear unwell.
Cause: The most common cause is bladder stones *(see Urolithiasis)*. Other causes include *Cystitis, Kidney Disease,* or *Tumours* of the bladder. Bloodstained urine in females may also be due to a problem in the womb or vagina.
Treatment: This depends on the cause of the problem. Fluids are needed for all cases, and if the hamster is not drinking, water or electrolytes should be given by mouth while the cause is investigated.

HAMSTER PLAGUE
An infectious disease, recognised relatively recently.
Signs: The hamster will be cold and lethargic, and becomes anorexic and dehydrated. Fits may follow and the disease can be fatal within 24 hours.
Cause: It is caused by a virus.
Treatment: There is no cure. Supportive nursing – keeping the patient warm, quiet, and providing plenty of fluids – may help, but is rarely successful.

HEAD TILT

A common symptom of disease in the inner ear or brain.

Signs: The head will be down on one side and balance may be affected. This onset may be sudden, or may progress gradually. There may also be an accompanying nystagmus (where the eyes flick from side to side) due to brain injury.

Cause: Head tilt is a symptom of middle ear disease, stroke, or the rare *Lymphocytic Choriomeningitis Virus (LCMV)*. Middle ear disease is normally caused by an infection, either following an infestation of *Ear Mites* or spread from *Respiratory Disease*.

Treatment: Middle ear infections are treated with antibiotics and anti-inflammatory drugs. If balance is affected, the hamster may have difficulty feeding and drinking, and nursing care will be required until the hamster recovers.

HEART DISEASE

Heart disease usually affects older hamsters. Hamsters can be born with a heart condition, but such individuals rarely survive.

Signs: Hamsters with heart disease become tired easily and take less exercise. They become short of breath after exercise and may collapse when climbing or using an exercise wheel. Breathing is laboured (faster and more obvious), and the extremities (i.e. feet, ears, and nose) can become cyanotic (coloured blue due to a lack of oxygenated blood). Sudden collapse and death can occur without previous symptoms.

Cause: Cardiac thrombosis is common, and females are generally affected at a younger age than males. Thrombosis can result from bacteria in the blood (e.g. from a previous respiratory infection) settling on a heart valve, which then fails to shut properly. *Amyloidosis* can also be a cause of thrombosis.

Treatment: Exercise should be limited. Hamsters with heart disease are best housed in a glass or plastic cage, where they cannot climb, and with no exercise wheel.

HEAT STROKE

When the hamster collapses from too much heat (also known as sleeper disease).

Signs: The hamster appears to be deeply asleep or dead, and will have wet, matted fur.

Cause: Hamsters are particularly susceptible to heat stroke when temperatures exceed 20 to 25 degrees Celsius (68 to 77 degrees Fahrenheit). Cages, particularly glass or plastic ones, should never be left in direct sunlight. Lack of water will also contribute to overheating in warm conditions.

Treatment: Pour cool water over the hamster to revive it, and then encourage it to drink. Extra fluids can be given by mouth or injection, if the hamster is significantly dehydrated. Dehydration caused by heat stroke can cause kidney failure.

HIBERNATION

An inactive or dormant state intended to preserve food by slowing all body functions.

Signs: The hamster appears deeply asleep or dead. Breathing is barely visible and the heart rate is slow. The hamster may feel cool to the touch.

Cause: This happens when the environmental temperature drops below 5 degrees

Celsius (41 degrees Fahrenheit). Older animals are more susceptible.

Treatment: The hamster should be warmed slowly in an airing cupboard or on a hot water bottle filled with warm (not boiling) water. A hairdryer can be used, but care must be taken not to burn the skin or overheat the hamster. It may take an hour to revive the hamster, and a drop of brandy can be given once the hamster is semi-conscious. Once revived, electrolytes, water, or milk mix should be given by dropper, to replace lost fluids, and the hamster should be kept in a warm, constant environment.

HIND LIMB PARALYSIS
Loss of use of one or both hind legs.

Signs: The hind legs become stiff, unable to move independently, and drag behind the hamster.

Cause: There is a similar condition known as *Cage Paralysis*, but this is not quite the same. True hind leg paralysis may be caused by an injury to the spine, which damages the nerves to the hind legs, or a hereditary condition in males that develops at 6 to 10 months.

Treatment: If the condition is caused by back injury, the best treatment is plenty of rest, with painkillers or anti-inflammatories (e.g. aspirin or steroids). There is no treatment for the condition, and affected lines should not be bred from.

HYPOTHYROIDISM
A deficiency of the thyroid hormone. This endocrine condition is thought to be uncommon in hamsters.

Signs: Lethargy and *Alopecia*.

Cause: A deficiency of thyroid hormone.

Treatment: Thyroid tablets for dogs can be broken up and given in small doses. Thyroid hormone improves hair growth even if *Alopecia* was not due to insufficient hormone levels. Therefore, a positive response to treatment does not necessarily confirm the diagnosis. It takes several weeks to see an improvement.

I

IMPACTED CHEEK POUCHES
Blocked cheek pouches.

Signs: A swollen face and neck with excess salivation and *Anorexia*.

Cause: Sticky foods (such as sweets, chocolate and artificial fibres) are the most common things to become impacted.

Treatment: The impacted material should be pulled out or flushed with water. A general anaesthetic may be required.

IMPACTION
See Constipation.

INFERTILITY
When repeated mating fails to produce offspring, the male or female is infertile. This may be temporary, particularly in the autumn (fall) and winter, or permanent.

Signs: No pregnancy after mating with different partners.

Cause: Obesity can cause infertility in male and female hamsters, as can insufficient dietary protein or vitamin E. Roborovski hamsters have higher protein requirements than other species of hamsters and are particularly susceptible to such nutritional deficiencies.

However, some causes of infertility are seasonal. Hamsters are seasonal breeders and become less fertile as the days become shorter, usually ceasing breeding altogether during winter months. When kept in colonies, submissive females may have reduced fertility as a natural consequence.

Low environmental temperatures may cause the male's testicles to be retracted, resulting in temporary infertility that should cease once temperatures warm up. Males can also become infertile from overuse. Some animals are permanently infertile, such as most albino Chinese hamsters. *Lymphocytic Choriomeningitis Virus (LCMV)* is a rare infection in hamsters, and one of the signs may be infertility.

Treatment: Weight loss can increase fertility in obese hamsters. Adding more green foods and encouraging exercise should help. Boiled egg, cheese and meat can all be added to the ration of breeding hamsters to increase protein levels, while vitamin E can be supplemented by sprinkling wheatgerm on food. Hamsters can be encouraged to breed in the winter by keeping the cage close to an electric light for 14 to 18 hours a day, and by maintaining a warm temperature. There is no treatment for infertility caused by *LCMV*.

INTUSSUSCEPTION
A serious condition where a piece of bowel telescopes inside itself, causing a partial or complete obstruction.

Signs: Affected animals are very miserable, suffering acute abdominal pain that causes them to sit hunched over or to hide away. There may be some bloody diarrhoea, or no faeces at all if the intussusception causes a complete obstruction. Straining can lead to *Rectal Prolapse*.

Cause: Intussusception normally follows a bout of diarrhoea or constipation, but anything that alters normal gut movement can lead to intussusception.

Treatment: Surgery can be attempted to straighten the bowel, although this is a delicate procedure in a very sick hamster. If the blood supply to the gut has been damaged, the affected portion must be removed. Euthanasia may be the preferred option.

J
No entries.

K

KIDNEY DISEASE
Kidney disease is common in hamsters, although many do not show any symptoms and survive with partially functioning kidneys.

Signs: There is an increased thirst and urine production *(see Polydipsia and Polyuria),* which may be accompanied by *Haematuria* (blood in the urine). The affected hamster will gradually lose weight, due to protein loss through the urine, but this may not be obvious initially, due to fluid retention causing a slightly swollen abdomen. Fluid retention (known as ascites) is also a sign of *Heart Disease* and *Liver Disease*. A simple dipstick test is used on a few drops of urine to check for protein. *Alopecia* is often associated with kidney failure in older hamsters, as are sticky eyes. *Cause: Amyloidosis* is a major cause of kidney disease in hamsters, particularly females. Kidney failure is also a common sequel to heat stroke. Left untreated, *Cystitis* can spread to the kidneys and result in kidney failure.

Treatment: Fresh, clean water should always be available. Hamsters with kidney failure produce large quantities of dilute urine and drink more than normal in response.

If they do not drink to replace the fluid, dehydration leads to further damage and illness. It may help to feed a reduced-protein diet, by replacing some of the dry food with cooked rice or a little cereal.

Water-soluble vitamins are lost in the urine, so a vitamin supplement can be added to the drinking water or food.

L

LIVER DISEASE
When disease or illness prevents the liver from functioning fully.

Signs: Mild liver disease has few signs, other than the hamster appearing to be generally out of condition. Progression of the disease leads to weight loss, ascites (the abdomen becomes swollen with fluid), and sometimes *Polydipsia and Polyuria,* and *Diarrhoea.* Severe liver damage can cause jaundice, in which case the whole body will be tinted yellow. This is particularly noticeable in the whites of the eyes and in the mouth.

Cause: Liver disease can be caused by infections, or, more commonly, *Amyloidosis. Tumours* (both primary and secondary) are another major cause.

Treatment: If infection is suspected, antibiotics can be given. Otherwise, treatment is supportive (to ease symptoms), rather than curative. Fluids and vitamins should be given and the diet should be easily digestible.

LYMPHOCYTIC CHORIOMENINGITIS VIRUS (LCMV)
A zoonotic disease (i.e. can be passed to humans) of mice that can also be carried by hamsters. Currently, it is not thought to be present in UK hamsters. In the US and Germany, it has been well documented in humans who have caught it from hamsters. It causes flu-like symptoms in humans, and occasionally a fatal encephalomyelitis (brain disease).

Signs: There are usually no symptoms, although it can cause *Pyometra, Head Tilt, Paralysis, Fits, Conjunctivitis* and *Infertility.*

Cause: The virus is spread in saliva, faeces, urine, and milk from other hamsters, or, more likely, from wild rodents. Infected mice have been found at various sites in the UK.

Treatment: There is no treatment. However, because it is a zoonotic disease, all affected and in-contact rodents should be humanely destroyed. Hamsters should be kept in a secure room, where wild rodents cannot gain entry, to protect against this and other diseases.

M

MALOCCLUSION

Hamsters' teeth, like all rodents, never stop growing. If the teeth do not meet each other, this is termed malocclusion. It causes problems when the teeth do not wear down and so become overlong.

Signs: Dribbling, difficulty in eating, or *Anorexia* in severe cases.

Cause: Malocclusion can be congenital, but, more often than not, it is due to a broken tooth, caused by a fall or by gnawing on the cage bars. Low calcium in the diet weakens the teeth and makes them more susceptible to breakage.

Treatment: Overgrown teeth should be clipped. Hard foods or non-toxic wood (e.g. apple or oak) should be provided for the hamster to gnaw on. Dog biscuits are suitable as they are also high in calcium and phosphorus. If this fails to keep the teeth short, they will need regular clipping every few weeks.

MAMMARY TUMOURS

Tumours of the mammary gland (breast cancer), usually malignant, although benign (non-spreading) tumours can occur.

Signs: Swelling of one or more mammary glands, sometimes associated with a discharge from the nipple. Normally, the area is not painful to touch.

Cause: Mammary tumours are invariably a primary cancer, and have not spread from elsewhere. However, once the tumours have developed in the glands, secondary tumours may develop elsewhere.

Treatment: Surgical removal of the affected gland or glands. Recurrence is common and malignant tumours can spread throughout the body.

MANGE

A skin condition causing irritation, hair loss and scurf. Two types of mite can infect hamsters *(see Acariasis, and Sarcoptic Mange)*.

MASTITIS

An infection of the mammary glands, usually during lactation.

Signs: Warm, swollen glands that may have a bloody or dark discharge from the nipples. The female will seem unwell and may cannibalise her litter.

Cause: Bacterial infection. Bacteria may enter the mammary glands through teat sores, which are caused by the teeth of the babies. This is more likely with a large litter or a poor milk supply.

Treatment: Antibiotics must be given promptly, and painkillers should be supplied by a vet.

MICROPHTHALMIA

A congenital condition where the eye is not properly formed. One or both eyes may be affected. The eye is smaller than normal, and part of the eyeball is obscured by the third eyelid, although there may be some sight from the exposed part of the eye. There is no treatment. Hamsters have poor sight generally, so they often cope very well with this condition.

N

No entries.

O

OBESITY

Overweight hamsters are more likely to be infertile and are more susceptible to fractures and dislocations caused by a fall. Obesity can also predispose the hamster to *Heart Disease* and *Cage Paralysis*.

Signs: Excess weight and a reluctance to exercise.

Cause: Lack of exercise and overfeeding. Hamsters fed a mixed diet may pick out their favourite bits, such as sunflower seeds, which are more fattening.

Treatment: Adjust the diet to include more greens and less concentrate. Avoid treats and encourage exercise by providing tunnels to explore, a wheel, or allowing the hamster to exercise, under supervision, out of its cage.

ORCHITIS

Inflammation of one or both testicles.

Signs: The affected testicle will be hot, swollen, and painful, and the hamster may be seen licking at it. If one side is affected only, it will initially appear larger than the other, although, in time, it will shrink, due to the build-up of scar tissue.

Cause: Trauma, such as a bite from another hamster, or bacteria from an infection elsewhere in the body, spread by the bloodstream.

Treatment: Antibiotics and anti-inflammatories, given by injection or in the food, are essential. *Castration* should be considered in unresponsive or recurring cases.

OVARIAN CYSTS

Cysts growing on the ovaries, which are relatively common in females that have never produced a litter.

Signs: There is a dark or bloody discharge from the vulva. Females used for breeding will develop abnormal cycles and are likely to become infertile. Cysts can grow so large that the whole abdomen will become enlarged and swollen.

Cause: Hormonal imbalances, or the effect of repeated cycles without pregnancy and lactation.

Treatment: Surgical removal of both ovaries and the womb, known as *Ovariohysterectomy* and commonly referred to as *Spaying*.

OVARIOHYSTERECTOMY

Surgical removal of womb and both ovaries, commonly called spaying.

It is usually carried out to treat cases of *Pyometra* or prolonged *Dystocia*, where the young are decayed. It is a major operation performed under general anaesthetic.

OVERGROWN TOENAILS

Older or obese hamsters are more likely to need regular clipping of their toenails, which do not wear down due to reduced exercise.

Small nail clippers are suitable for clipping. In light-coloured nails, the quick (the nail's blood and nerve supply) can be seen as a slightly darker line, and the nail should be cut a little beyond the end of this. Blood loss from accidentally cutting the quick is unlikely to be significant, but it will be painful, so do not be surprised if your hamster attempts to bite you. If bleeding does not stop relatively quickly, consult your vet.

P

PAPOVA VIRUS
Infection with Papova virus is associated with different *Tumours*.
Signs: Wart-like growths on the face are the most common symptom, but the virus can also cause fatal malignant lymphoma in young animals, which develops as rapidly growing, large internal growths.
Cause: The virus is caught from other hamsters and there may be a heritable link.
Treatment: There is no treatment. The wart-like growths are rarely a problem, but lymphoma is rapidly fatal. Affected individuals should be isolated immediately and culled from a breeding colony.

PARALYSIS
A partial or complete loss of sensation and movement.
Signs: Complete or partial inability to move. A hamster suffering from partial paralysis may drag its legs behind it when scrabbling around the cage.
Cause: Spinal trauma can damage the nerves to hind legs. If the neck is involved, the fore legs may also be affected. Two specific conditions causing paralysis are *Hind Limb Paralysis* and *Cage Paralysis.*
Treatment: Spinal trauma requires rest and steroids, and recovery may take some time.

PNEUMONIA
An infection of the lungs.
Pneumonia may develop if *Respiratory Infections* are not treated promptly. Often fatal.

POLYCYSTIC DISEASE
An uncommon developmental disease in which cysts develop in the hamster's body.
Signs: There are no outward clinical signs. Cysts are normally found incidentally, during surgery or post mortem, on hamsters older than one year. Cysts are found most often in the liver.
Cause: This is most likely to be a congenital defect.
Treatment: No treatment is necessary.

POLYURIA AND POLYDIPSIA
Polyuria is an increase in urine production, and polydipsia is an increase in thirst.
Both can be symptoms of many diseases such as *Diabetes, Cushing's Disease, Kidney Disease, Liver Disease and Pyometra.*

PSEUDOPREGNANCY
When a non-pregnant female displays the 'symptoms' of pregnancy.

Signs: The female does not come into oestrus (season) four days after mating, but nor does she develop a swollen abdomen or make a nest.

Cause: Pseudopregnancy follows an infertile mating.

Treatment: No treatment is necessary and she is likely to return to oestrus 12 to 14 days after mating.

PYOMETRA

An infection of the womb.

Signs: Pyometra may be open or closed. In an open infection, there is a vaginal discharge through the cervix, which can be confused with a bladder problem if the pus is washed out at urination. In a closed pyometra, there is no discharge. The abdomen will be swollen in both cases, as the womb fills with pus at least as big as the size of a pregnancy.

Toxins from the infection make the hamster feel unwell, which will be accompanied by increased thirst and decreased appetite. The condition is invariably fatal if untreated.

Cause: Infection can spread to the womb from a *Respiratory Infection*, such as the *Streptococcus* species and *Pasteurella pneumotropica* bacteria. *Lymphocytic Chorio-meningitis Virus (LCMV)* is another cause. If parturition (birth) is incomplete, so that a dead baby or some afterbirth are left behind in the womb, this will lead to pyometra if the hamster survives the initial *Dystocia*. Pyometra can also occur due to no apparent reason.

Treatment: Antibiotic treatment can produce a temporary improvement but is highly unlikely to cure the condition. *Ovariohysterectomy* is the only cure. Although surgery is delicate, and the anaesthetic risk is increased in a sick hamster, many vets have performed this successfully. Very recently, some vets have found the drug Galastop to be effective.

No entries.

RABIES

Hamsters, like all warm-blooded mammals, are susceptible to rabies.

Signs: Initial signs include 'dullness' and changes in temperament, leading to the hamster becoming excitable and aggressive. Convulsions and death follow in a short space of time.

Cause: Rabies is caused by a virus carried in the saliva of infected animals and usually passed on by a bite. This is probably why reports of rabies-affected hamsters in countries that have the virus are rare – the hamster does not survive the bite!

Treatment: There is no treatment and death is inevitable. Rabies is a zoonotic disease (can be passed to humans), so hamsters are currently subjected to quarantine of six months if entering the UK from rabies-infected countries. There are proposals to include them, and other small pets, in the UK pet passport system, which would allow them to be taken abroad and to return without quarantine. However, these proposals have not been finalised.

In America, hamsters are not subject to rabies legislation. However, the presence of anti-vermin laws in some states (see page 11) directly affects hamsters, so care should be taken before importing a hamster to the US.

RECTAL PROLAPSE

When part of the rectum collapses and protrudes from the anus. It is usually a sequel to another disease.

Signs: A red swelling protruding from the anus.

Cause: Usually follows a bout of *Diarrhoea* or an *Intussusception*.

Treatment: The prolapse must be cleaned and gently replaced by a vet, which may require a general anaesthetic. Fluids should be given until the hamster is eating normally.

RESPIRATORY INFECTION

Infections of the upper and lower airways. This is the second most common disease in hamsters (after Diarrhoea).

Signs: Sneezing, with a discharge from the nose and eyes. Breathing is laboured, often faster than normal, and a 'rattly' chest noise may be heard. Affected hamsters will have a dull coat and will be generally miserable and lethargic, sitting hunched over. They may be seen shivering and are usually *Anorexic*. If the infection is not treated promptly, *Pneumonia* may develop, leading to severe breathing difficulty and often death.

Cause: A variety of bacteria and viruses can be the cause, some of which may be caught from humans – hamsters can catch the human strains of colds and flu, as well as the *Streptococcus* bacteria that cause sore throats in people. *Sendai* virus is another cause of pneumonia, albeit rare. *Pasteurella* bacteria are carried by many healthy hamsters, normally without problems, but can cause respiratory disease at times of stress.

Sneezing and runny eyes may be a sign of an *Allergy,* but if the hamster is unwell, veterinary advice should be sought.

Treatment: Veterinary treatment should be sought promptly as antibiotics are needed to treat or prevent pneumonia. The patient should be kept in a warm, constant environment and given plenty of fluids. A warm water-and-milk mix (50:50) will help to give the hamster some energy. Vapour rub can help to clear the airways and can be dabbed around the cage or applied to the hamster's chest with a cotton wool (cotton) bud. A small dose (one drop) of a human decongestant can also be given. To prevent respiratory problems, hamsters should be kept in a room with a constant temperature – not in a room such as a hallway, which becomes much colder at night. Children with colds and sore throats are an infection risk to hamsters, so should avoid contact with them until recovered.

RINGWORM

A fungal infection of the skin.

Signs: Hair loss with a dry, flaky, often yellow-tinged skin. The hamster may also be pruritic (itchy).

Cause: A fungus that burrows into the skin and hair follicles on the body and ears. Ringworm is not an actual worm but, because the affected areas sometimes look as if there is a roundworm burrowing in the skin, the fungus is given the name of ringworm. There are several strains of ringworm that can infect hamsters, and some can also infect other species, including people. The fungus breeds in damp conditions, which is why care must be taken when housing hamsters in enclosed plastic cages. Hair samples need to be taken to confirm ringworm.

Treatment: Treatment consists of regular bathing in an iodine-based shampoo, which should also be used to wash the cage. Specific anti-fungal shampoos are also available. Longhaired hamsters need clipping before bathing, so that treatment can penetrate into the hair roots.

Two to three baths will be needed, at three-day intervals. Hamsters should be dried thoroughly after bathing, initially with a towel, and then with a hairdryer set to its lowest setting.

Anti-fungal drugs used on dogs, cats and larger animals may be used, but, because these have side effects, they are used only if bathing is unsuccessful.

To prevent a recurrence, ventilation in the cage, particularly in the nest box, should be improved.

S

SALMONELLOSIS
An infection of *Salmonella* bacteria. This is a zoonotic infection (i.e. it can be transmitted to people).

Signs: Severe *Salmonella* infections will lead to acute illness, with symptoms of *Anorexia* and *Diarrhoea,* which may result in death. Milder forms will have symptoms of lethargy and *Weight Loss*.

Cause: There are two types of *Salmonella* bacteria that infect hamsters, called *Salmonella enteritidis* and *Salmonella typhimurium*. They are excreted in the faeces of carrier animals and can infect food or bedding. Contamination of food or water, with faeces from wild rodents or birds carrying the bacteria, is a likely source of infection.

Treatment: Supportive treatment for *Diarrhoea* is based on fluids, warmth, and general nursing. Antibiotics are not generally prescribed because any hamster that survives the infection is likely to become a carrier of the disease, and may spread the disease. Cages should be thoroughly cleaned and disinfected, and hands washed well in disinfectant soap.

SARCOPTIC MANGE
A contagious skin disease caused by a tiny parasite living on the skin.

Signs: Hair loss on the body, particularly on the face. This is pruritic (itchy) and can spread between hamsters. Affected areas are scurfy with small scabs.

Cause: A mite called *Sarcoptes scabeii,* which is too small to see but burrows into the skin. Scrapings from the skin need to be examined under a microscope to confirm diagnosis.

Treatment: A drug called Ivermectin (more commonly used to worm cattle) is effective. This can be given by injection but is more often prescribed as drops to be given in the mouth every 7 to 10 days. All hamsters that have been in contact with the parasite should be treated and their cages cleaned. The mite can live in bedding and hair for several days.

SATINISATION
A particular type of shiny coat produced in hamsters with the satin gene.
When hamsters carrying the satin gene are mated to each other, the offspring have a thin coat known as supersatinisation. Breeding of supersatins results in offspring that are virtually bald.

SCURF
Scurfy or flaky skin can be due to a variety of conditions.
Signs: Depending on the cause, there may be pruritis (itching) and *Alopecia* (hair loss), as well as a dry, flaky coat.
Cause: Demodex or *Sarcoptic Mange* mites, and *Ringworm* are common causes. *Allergies* from diet or bedding, and dietary imbalances, can also be causes.
Treatment: The underlying cause must be treated, General skin and coat condition will often improve by supplementing the daily diet with one or two drops of cod liver oil, and some vitamin A and D, in a crumbled yeast tablet.

SKIN SORES
Broken areas of the skin, which can become infected and develop into abscesses if left untreated.
Signs: Open wounds on the skin, particularly on the legs, face, and scent glands.
Cause: Sores can result when a hamster rubs its face or body against a hard surface, or licks and grooms itself excessively. Legs may develop sores from the bars of an exercise wheel if the wheel is not completely solid. Water escaping from a leaky water bottle may dribble onto the hamster's chin and cause sores. Males will sometimes lick their scent glands to such an extent that they develop sore patches on each flank.
Treatment: The cause of the sores (e.g. any sharp or abrasive surfaces) should be found and eliminated. An open-barred exercise wheel should be replaced with a solid one, or lined with cardboard. Affected areas on the hamster's body should be cleaned with salt water or a diluted antiseptic, and treated with a soothing antiseptic cream. In rare cases, some males are incapable of stopping themselves from licking their scent glands. If treatment and isolation (the sight and smells of other hamsters can stimulate scent gland licking) fails, *Castration* may be used as a last resort.

SPAYING
See Ovariohysterectomy.

STILLBIRTH
When one or more babies from a litter are born dead. The term Stillbirth is reserved for babies born after, or close to, the normal gestation period. Babies born too early, or babies that seem to have been dead for a couple of days before birth (so that they have begun to decay), are considered to have been naturally aborted.
Signs: One or more babies from a litter seem normally formed but are dead.
Cause: Hamsters are seasonal breeders, and winter breeding often results in stillbirths. Vitamin E deficiency can also cause this. Older hamsters reaching the end of their reproductive life are more likely to have stillborn young.
Treatment: Adding extra vitamin E to the diet, and maintaining a warm environment with 12 to 14 hours of light (to mimic summer) may help.

STROKE

A blood clot in the brain that, depending on the severity, can affect balance and movement, and may cause death. Elderly hamsters are normally affected.

Signs: Mild strokes may cause the hamster to walk to one side, with *Head Tilt*. The eyes may flick rapidly from side to side, known as nystagmus. In more severe cases, there may be a complete loss of balance, and the hamster may collapse and die.

Cause: Strokes are caused by a blood clot on the brain, which may be brought on by head injury.

Treatment: Anti-inflammatory drugs, such as cortisone, help prevent further brain damage from swelling. Fluids and food may need to be given by hand for a few days. Recovery is variable and takes several days. There may be permanent damage.

T

TEETH

Hamsters' teeth (like all rodents) have open roots, so never stop growing. The teeth are naturally yellow, and the colour becomes stronger with age. If the teeth are not evenly worn, *Malocclusion* can result. Chewing on cage bars may break teeth, as can falls. Broken teeth can lead to further problems and infections, and dental *Caries* are common in hamsters.

TESTICULAR CANCER

A hamster's testicles are always prominent but can become larger due to infection (See *Orchitis)* or *Tumours/Neoplasia* (cancer).

Signs: Tumours usually affect one testicle only, which becomes noticeably larger than the other. The affected testicle may produce hormones that make the hamster more aggressive, or sometimes more feminine.

Cause: Tumours are usually primary.

Treatment: Castration is the only cure. It is possible to remove the affected testicle only, if the hamster is used for breeding, although the other testicle is often left infertile, at least temporarily.

TUMOURS/NEOPLASIA

A tumour is a swelling of abnormal tissue, and a neoplasm is a new growth. They may be benign, which means they do not spread and are generally slower growing, or they can be malignant. Malignant tumours are faster growing and able to spread elsewhere in the body, and these are referred to as cancerous. Benign tumours can also grow very large and become a physical problem.

Signs: External tumours are visible as firm lumps that are not usually painful to touch. Internal tumours may be large enough to cause abdominal swelling, otherwise symptoms will vary depending on which organs are affected.

Cause: Many types of tumour have no known cause. Viruses, such as the *Papova Virus*, can cause tumours, but many are caused by hereditary factors, particularly in Dwarf Russian hamsters.

Treatment: Even large tumours can be successfully removed by surgery. However, many recur, sometimes quickly and sometimes after a long absence. If tumours are thought to be hereditary, or associated with the *Papova Virus,* affected lines should not be bred from.

TYZZER'S DISEASE
A condition, more often seen in mice, which may be seen in weaning hamsters or stressed individuals, particularly those kept in the same room as mice.
Signs: Diarrhoea, leading to dehydration and death within 24 hours. Occasionally, the disease may take a milder form, manifesting as chronic weight loss.
Cause: An organism called *Bacillus piliformis*, the spores of which live in soil, bedding or contaminated food for up to one year.
Treatment: Treatment is rarely successful. Fluids should be given every hour, by mouth or injection, and the patient should be kept warm and dry. Antibiotics (such as oxytetracycline) can be given to hamsters that have been in contact with the organism, to control the spread of the disease, but Tyzzer's Disease has such a rapid onset that antibiotics are unlikely to help the affected individual.

U
UROLITHIASIS
The technical term for bladder stones.
Signs: The only sign may be blood in the urine *(see Haematuria)*. The hamster may also show signs of discomfort from the stones, and display the symptoms of *Cystitis*. Increased thirst and urination *(see Polydipsia and Polyuria)* may be other symptoms. If the stones block the bladder, the abdomen will become swollen and painful. There may be some dribbling of urine but no normal urination. Large stones can be felt under examination; otherwise, a radiograph (X-ray) will confirm their presence.
Cause: Hamster urine naturally contains small crystals. When these form large clumps, bladder stones are the result. This is more likely in concentrated urine, and some hamsters seem particularly susceptible.
Treatment: Surgical removal of the stones is the only treatment, and not necessarily a permanent cure, as stones commonly recur. Altering the diet may help to prevent their formation, and hamsters should be encouraged to drink plenty of fluids to flush crystals from the bladder. Fresh, clean water should always be available.

V
VITAMIN DEFICIENCIES
Hamsters rely on *Coprophagy* for their full vitamin intake. If this is affected, or if the diet is deficient in some way, a variety of vitamin deficiencies can occur. Vitamin E deficiency, which is one of the more common deficiencies, causes stiffness and may even lead to death. Wheat germ can be added to the diet as a source of vitamin E, and a multivitamin supplement given in the water may also help.

W
WARTS
Small, benign growths caused by a virus.
Warts often disappear after a few months, meaning that veterinary intervention is not always needed. If warts become a problem (e.g. if they are in an awkward place, or if they become infected or sore), they can be surgically removed by a vet.

WEIGHT LOSS

Weight loss may be accompanied by *Anorexia* or may occur despite a normal appetite.

Signs: Mild weight loss may not be noticeable, due to the large amount of loose skin covering the body. In moderate to severe cases, the ribs will be more prominent.

Cause: The most common cause is teeth problems *(see Malocclusion)*. *Liver Disease*, *Kidney Disease* and *Diabetes* are also causes. In some cases, weight loss can be the first symptom of more rare conditions, such as *Yersinia* and *Salmonella*.

Treatment: The teeth should be examined and clipped if necessary. Further tests may be required to diagnose other diseases before appropriate treatment can be given.

WET TAIL

A term used to describe often-fatal diarrhoea, caused by a range of bacteria and usually associated with stress. It is also known by the technical terms Proliferative Ileitis and Transmissable Ileal Hyperplasia. The ileum is the affected part of the small intestine.

Signs: Severe watery diarrhoea, which results in soiling of the tail and rear end (hence the term 'wet tail'). The hamster will appear unwell, hunched, *Anorexic,* and lethargic. Wet tail commonly leads to death within a few days.

Cause: There is no specific cause, rather a variety of factors and infectious agents are responsible. The bacteria *E.coli* and *Campylobacter* species have been found in many cases, but they have also been found in healthy hamsters. It is likely these bacteria combine, causing disease after a time of stress when the body's immune system is weakened. Stress triggers include weaning, moving to a new home, malnutrition, and overcrowding. The disease is more common in longhaired varieties and uncommon in Dwarf hamsters.

Treatment: Affected animals should be isolated, as wet tail can be contagious. Supportive treatment, particularly the provision of fluids, should begin immediately. Specific antibiotics may be prescribed along with an injection of multivitamins. Dehydration rapidly leads to shock and hypothermia, so sufferers must be kept warm. Shock may be treated by a vet with an injection of corticosteroids. Many cases are fatal, despite treatment. Good hygiene is essential for prevention, as is minimising stressful situations. Antibiotics in the drinking water may be prescribed to prevent spread within a group. If an outbreak occurs, bedding should be destroyed and the cage, nest boxes, food dishes and water bottles should be thoroughly cleaned and disinfected.

WORMS

Both tapeworms and pinworms can infect hamsters. The tapeworms can also be passed to humans. Protozoa are not strictly worms but are similar parasites of the intestines.

Signs: Infestation with pin or tapeworms is common without clinical signs. Tapeworms may cause weight loss and mild *Diarrhoea*. Heavy infestations can cause *Constipation* or *Impaction*, while heavy infestations of the protozoa *Hexamita* or *Giardia* cause *Diarrhoea, Weight Loss*, and even death.

Cause: The tapeworm *Hymnenolepis nana* is picked up from the faeces of an infested rodent, or from beetles or fleas. Pinworms are spread in the faeces of infested rodents. Hamsters can contract the mouse pinworm *Syphacia obvelata* or the rat type

Syphacia muris. Tapeworm eggs or protozoa are found by examining faeces under a microscope, and egg samples can be collected on sticky-tape from around the anus, which are then examined under a microscope also.

Treatment: For tapeworms, the drug niclosamide is given by mouth, with the treatment repeated one week later. There are preparations for dogs that can be measured to the correct dose. Pinworms are killed by piperazine, given by mouth every day for one week. Wild rodents and insects should be kept out of the environment and the cages should be cleaned regularly to prevent infestation. Adding the drug metronidazole to the hamster's food should kill protozoa. Your vet will prescribe the appropriate treatment and dose.

WOUNDS

Fighting is common, and wounds may be severe.

Signs: Wounds may be hidden in the coat, and only a little blood may show on the surface. Male hamsters may be bitten on the testicles when fighting.

Cause: Fighting or injury on other objects. *Skin Sores* are common leg wounds that occur when the hamster rubs itself against the bars of its exercise wheel.

Treatment: Wounds should be thoroughly cleaned. The hamster may suffer from shock, so should be kept warm and quiet. Giving a little honey and water by mouth will provide energy to keep warm. Deep or bruised wounds may need antibiotics to prevent infection. Castration may be necessary if the testicles are damaged.

X

No entries.

Y

YERSINIA

An infectious (uncommon) cause of *Diarrhoea* that is zoonotic.

Signs: Anorexia, Diarrhoea and *Weight loss.* Acute forms may cause sudden death.

Cause: A bacteria called *Yersinia pseudotuberculosis*, spread by wild birds and rodents, or by feeding green food that has been contaminated with bird droppings. A faecal sample needs to be sent to a laboratory to isolate the bacteria for diagnosis.

Treatment: General nursing, as used in cases of *Diarrhoea*. However, great care must be taken because of the risk posed to humans. Bedding must be destroyed and cages rigorously cleaned and disinfected. The hamster should not be handled without gloves. The disease can be prevented by ensuring that wild birds, rats, and mice cannot gain access to the hamster's environment.

Z

ZOONOSIS

A disease that can be transmitted to humans.

Zoonotic diseases of hamsters include *Ringworm, Tyzzer's Disease, Yersinia, Salmonella, Rabies, Tapeworm* and the *Lymphocytic Choriomeningitis Virus (LCMV).*

CHAPTER 10

BREEDING SYRIAN HAMSTERS

1. The breeding pair
2. Mating
3. Pregnancy and birth
4. The nursing mother
5. The babies
6. Separating mother and babies
7. Fostering and hand-rearing
8. Record keeping
9. Colours and patterns
10. Simple genetics
11. Colour combinations

Female Syrian hamsters may have 15 or more babies in a litter, although the average is 6 to 10. They normally make excellent mothers, giving birth and raising their litters with few problems, but the numbers in a litter can make homing the offspring difficult. If you are seriously interested in breeding a litter, consider what outlets there may be for any of the babies that you do not intend to keep. A local pet shop may be interested in taking some of the babies, but it is best to check this out before you mate your hamsters, as it will be too late afterwards. If you are a member of a hamster club you may be able to sell your babies at one of their shows; and it is possible, with Syrian hamsters, to time the mating so that the litter is the correct age for a particular show. However, before you mate your hamsters, you should check that the show organisers are happy for you to sell the babies at their show. You will also need to be sure that the buyer is well suited to caring for a hamster, and this is not always easy to determine in a show environment.

If, after serious consideration, you decide to go ahead and breed from your hamsters, the rewards of seeing the babies grow and their characters developing are enormous, and there is much to enjoy.

1. THE BREEDING PAIR

Before deciding to breed from your hamsters, you should give some consideration to your hamsters' temperaments. Not only will the babies inherit their colour and build from their parents, but they may also inherit their parents' temperaments. You should breed from healthy, good-natured hamsters only, as this will help to produce healthy and placid babies.

FEMALE
Any female used for breeding should be a minimum of 13 weeks old. If she is younger than this, there may be problems during the pregnancy or you may end up with a very large litter. The maximum age for a female's first litter is eight months; any older could also lead to problems. We prefer to mate our hamsters between four and six months for the first litter, the age dependent on the female's size, build and condition. If we consider a female a little small, we would leave her to mature a little more, up to the age of six months.

MALE
The male's age is not as important as the female's, as long as he is sexually mature and of a size to be able to mate. However, if the male is too young, he may show no interest in the female, while if he is too old, he may no longer be fertile.

PAIRINGS TO AVOID
Any male will normally mate with any female, but this is not always desirable – certain pairings can lead to deformities in the babies. There are three main combinations of parents to avoid, to ensure deformities do not occur.

SATIN COATED
Do not mate a satin coat to a satin coat. This can lead to double satinisation, which results in a hamster with very sparse, very fine fur, and, in extreme cases, no fur whatsoever. A satin hamster should always be mated to a non-satin hamster, which normally produces a mixture of satin and non-satin babies, although there have been cases where the litter contains all satin babies or no satin babies.

WHITE BELLIED
Never mate two hamsters that carry the 'white-bellied' gene (the eyeless white gene). This combination can produce eyeless whites, which, as the name suggests, are white hamsters with rudimentary eyes or no eyes at all. All hamsters carrying this gene have white belly fur, but not all hamsters with white belly fur carry the gene. Not only is this confusing, it also makes it very difficult to separate carriers from non-carriers.

You should remember that banded and spotted hamsters have white belly fur, and unless you are 100 per cent certain that they are not carriers of the gene, it is best to mate them to a plain-coloured animal with normal-coloured belly fur.

All roan hamsters are carriers of the gene, so never mate a roan to another roan under any circumstances. A roan must always be mated to a plain-coloured animal with normal-coloured belly fur.

Some normal-coloured animals may carry the gene, but their white belly fur makes them easily identifiable. All carriers of the gene can also be identified by their eyes, which will shine with a bright-red glint when a strong light is shone into them. If you are in any doubt about whether both of your breeding pair carry the gene, play safe and do not mate them.

112

KINKED TAILS

Do not mate any hamster with a physical deformity, such as a 'kinked' tail. You can detect a kinked tail by running your thumb and forefinger down the length of the tail, although the kink may be obvious to the naked eye in extreme cases.

A kinked tail is usually found in the 'delicate' colours, although hamsters of all colours can have this condition. The term 'delicate' refers to those hamsters with a genetic predisposition to the kinked tail defect, rather than the actual shade of colour. Dark Grey, Lilac and Smoke Pearl are usually included among these colours. In the normal course of life, a kinked tail will make no difference to the health of the hamster, but, over time, breeding hamsters with kinked tails could produce offspring with congenital spinal problems. To be safe, it is wise not to use such hamsters for breeding purposes at all.

As hamster breeders, we often breed from our 'delicate' hamsters. However, to make sure we do not breed hamsters with defects, we are careful to out-cross our animals with 'stronger' colours in their genetic make-up. For example, every couple of generations we would mate Lilac to Cinnamon, Dark Grey to Golden, and Smoke Pearl to Yellow. The resulting offspring would be Cinnamon, Golden and Yellow respectively, but would also carry the 'delicate' colour gene, so that when they are mated to Lilac, Dark Grey or Smoke Pearl, the offspring produced would be of the desired 'delicate' colours.

Not all hamsters are born with a kinked tail due to genetic inheritance. Sometimes, a kinked tail can be the result of a fall, or may suddenly appear when the hamster is two to three months old. In either case, we would hesitate to use this animal for breeding. It should also be noted that any hamster with a kinked tail would almost certainly be disqualified from exhibition at a full hamster show.

2. MATING

Female hamsters normally come into season or 'on heat' every fourth day, approximately between sunset and sunrise. The later in the evening, the more likely the female is to be receptive. At any other time (the other three nights of the season), the female is likely to attack the male and injuries can occur if they are not separated quickly.

In their natural habitat, hamsters breed during spring and summer, to ensure maximum survival of their offspring. In the early days of hamster keeping, breeding took place during these spring and summer months only. However, nowadays it is possible to breed all year through, although to do this it is necessary to 'fool' the female hamster into believing that it is the correct time of year. This can be achieved by exposing the hamster to at least 12 hours of light a day, and also by providing a source of heat during the winter months.

We have found that supplying our males with regular (i.e. every other day) fresh greens has greatly improved the success rate of mating. Obviously, females can be fed the fresh greens as well. Since we introduced this routine to our hamstery, we have had almost 100 per cent mating success.

INTRODUCING THE PAIR

Unlike mice, gerbils, and rats, which can be left together to let nature take its course, male and female Syrian hamsters, which should be housed separately at all other times, must be introduced to each other under careful supervision. This is best done on neutral territory, or in the male's cage. Under no circumstances should the male be introduced into the female's cage. A container or box, measuring at least 24 x 18 inches (60 x 45 cms) and a minimum of 12 inches (30 cms) high, is ideal to use as a mating area. This allows some space for free movement but is small enough to ensure easy intervention should the female turn aggressively on the male.

It is best to try the mating late in the evening. Place the male and the female in the box and watch their behaviour and posture. If the female is not on heat, she may appear to be squatting, or trying to turn the male on his back by putting her nose under his belly. The male normally makes no effort to defend himself, so, before the female causes him any injury, the pair should be separated. During this initial stage of mating, it is wise to wear a glove on one hand. The gloved hand can be used to separate the pair if any aggression is shown, without receiving any bites on your bare hand. Once parted, the pair can be returned to their respective cages and the mating tried again the next night.

MATING

If the female is receptive she will run away for a few strides, but, when the male touches her back with his front paws, she will freeze. She will stand very still with her hind legs braced and her tail and ears erect. Once seen, this 'freezing' posture is always recognisable. Following this, the male will normally wash the female's rear end for a short time and then mount her from the rear by climbing partially onto her back. He will hold himself in place by gripping her around the middle with his front paws, and he may grip her neck fur with his teeth. Each individual act of mating lasts only a few seconds, with the male thrusting himself strongly into the female, sometimes finishing with a slight shudder. The male will then dismount and may wash himself and his partner before remounting.

The mating pair can be left together for between 20 and 30 minutes after the male is seen to penetrate. The act of mating will be repeated many times. Once mating has started, it is normally trouble-free, but the pair should never be unsupervised. Occasionally, the male may be overaggressive in biting the back of the female's neck, too enthusiastic about washing her ears, or trying to mount the wrong end. Touching the male will normally stop these occurrences. If the male seems to lose interest after 15 minutes, the pair should be separated and returned to their own cages. The same applies should the female begin to show aggressive tendencies towards the male.

MATING PROBLEMS

If the female freezes but the male shows no strong interest, it may be a little early in the evening for successful mating. Separate the pair and try again a couple of hours later. Young males may take a little longer to discover what is required of them, even though they get extremely excited in the presence of the female. They may try to mount from all directions, trying the patience of the female. It is always worthwhile to give a young male a few more minutes than an older one, before separating the pair.

If there is no response later in the evening, it might be beneficial to try the mating in the male's cage, first ensuring that you can quickly separate them in the event of things going awry (e.g. remove all the toys from the male's cage). An alternative male may need to be considered should all these methods fail, or you could try the same pair four days later.

A 'test' mating could be tried on the fourth night after the initial mating, to ensure the mating was successful. However, the female is likely to turn very quickly on the male if she is pregnant. If the female does not stand following mating, it is a good indication that she is pregnant, although it is not necessarily true in all cases. If she stands, mating can be tried again immediately.

3. PREGNANCY AND BIRTH

The gestation period for Syrian hamsters is 16 days, one of the shortest periods known in mammals. Consequently, great care should be taken when handling the female for the first seven days after a successful mating. In the later stages of pregnancy, it is a good idea to provide the female with some milk, either in the form of runny porridge, or bread soaked in milk. Giving a few extra sunflower seeds a day or two before the birth may also help milk production.

Two days before the babies are due, the female's cage should be cleaned and provided with plenty of fresh bedding to make a nest. After the female has given birth, the cage should not be cleaned again until the babies are two weeks old, although fresh food and water should be provided at regular intervals, and old, uneaten food should be discarded.

The babies may be born between midday on the 16th day, and the evening of the 17th day, with most arriving during the night of the 16th day. If, by the morning of the 18th day, the babies have not arrived, consult your vet.

The babies are born naked and blind, with their ears flat against their heads. Immediately following birth, the mother will normally lick them clean and then allow them to suckle. When all the babies have been born, the mother will wash herself thoroughly. Do not be surprised if you notice a little blood on the bedding following the birth; this is normal. However, if bleeding persists, or if the mother seems unwell, consult your vet.

4. THE NURSING MOTHER

For the first few days 'mum' will rarely leave the nest, except to collect food, drink, and to go to the toilet. When she leaves the nest, she will emerge very slowly, using the bedding material to scrape the babies from her teats. When she returns to the nest, you may hear some little squeaks as she settles. If she is startled, and runs from the nest hurriedly, the babies may be scattered outside the nest. Do not be tempted to return the babies to the nest as most mothers will do so themselves in a very short time. If the mother shows no sign of retrieving her stranded baby, it will usually squeak quite loudly. If you feel you must return the baby to the nest, use a spoon instead of your hand, as it will not have your scent on it. The mother should be distracted while you return the baby, either by giving her some extra food or by putting her out to play.

The nursing mother should be given milky foods every day, but great care must be taken with the dish containing the milky food. Baby hamsters are very mobile from a surprisingly early age, easily capable of wandering into a deep food dish. If a baby finds its way into a food dish full of milky food, and is unable to get out again, it will drown in a very short space of time.

COVERING BABIES

Many nursing mothers cover their babies every time they leave the nest. If your female Syrian is one of them, you must resist the temptation to open the nest to look at the babies. If the mother senses any interference, she may destroy her babies. However, if she leaves the nest open, feel free to look but do not touch the babies or upset the mother. It was 10 days before we managed a good look at our first litter! Some mothers will heap shavings around the nest as well as using the bedding to cover the babies. This is perfectly natural behaviour, but keep an eye on the amount of shavings and bedding used. Some mothers heap so much shavings and bedding on the nest that the babies may be in danger of suffocation. If you are worried about this, remove a little of the excess bedding and shavings.

INFANTICIDE

Many stories are heard of mums killing and eating their babies, but these are rare events. If you follow the guidelines in this book you should never experience this, although some of the babies may die through natural causes. Unfortunately, not all babies will survive. Some will be born with fatal deformities, others may catch a chill and die. If this happens, it is not unusual for the mother to dispose of the body by eating it. This, although repugnant to us, is instinctive to the mother; in a hamster's natural habitat a decaying baby would attract predators and endanger the rest of the family. However, the mother will not always eat her deceased young, and if you notice (usually by the smell) that a mum has tucked a dead baby away behind the nest, remove it when she is otherwise distracted in another part of the cage. Moving the food dish away from the nest and adding some new food to it can accomplish this.

MOTHERING INSTINCT

For most females, motherhood is instinctive. However, a very 'people-minded' hamster, or a highly inquisitive one, may leave the newborn babies alone in the nest for far too long at any given time. The tiny, naked babies will lose heat quickly, and, if they are not kept warm, they could die. If the female is absent from the nest for long periods, position the cage in a quiet place so that distractions are kept to a minimum. This may also be necessary if, every time you approach the cage, the mother rushes out to see you without carefully detaching the babies from her teats, scattering them in a trail from nest to cage bars. However, as the babies grow older and more self-sufficient, do not be surprised if even a good mother leaves her babies alone for longer periods.

5. THE BABIES

Baby hamsters grow very quickly. Fur starts to grow quite early, and, by the seventh day, dark-coloured babies can be distinguished from light. The babies' eyes will be firmly closed at this time, but you may be able to detect whether the hamster's eyes are red or black through the eyelids. Surprisingly, at this age it is even possible to sex the babies, as the teats of the females are visible.

7 TO 14 DAYS

From the seventh day onwards, you can start introducing a little solid food, as the babies' teeth have started growing by this time. An ideal mix can be made from wheat germ, first-stage dried baby food, and small, broken particles of hamster food. The mix should be sprinkled into the nest for the babies to eat. However, it is best to put a teaspoonful in mum's dish, otherwise she will consume the babies' share.

At around 10 days old, the babies may try to eat the mother's milky food. Consequently, you must use a very shallow dish for the milky food, so that the babies are not in danger of drowning. As the babies grow, some mothers will let them wander and gather food for themselves, while others will retrieve them if they stray too far from the nest. Growing babies need to eat a lot of food, so, if the mother is one who does not let her babies venture out too far, it is advisable to drop a handful of extra food into the nest.

At 10 days, patterning may be visible, especially if the babies are dark in colour. Between 10 and 14 days, most colours will become evident, and the babies' eyes will start to open. If you are hoping for Golden or Dark Grey hamsters in the litter you will have to wait a little longer to see if these colours have bred true. It may be as late as 14 to 15 days before these colours can be positively identified, although they will be become obvious virtually overnight. The offspring may not always be the colour you would expect, unless you know the full background of the parents, but whatever colour the babies turn out to be, raising a litter will have been great fun.

14 TO 21 DAYS

At 14 days, provided the mother is not too overprotective, you may be able to clean the wet corner, dispose of any old food and replace it with fresh supplies. However, you must take great care not to upset mum. It is advisable to put her out to play while you clean the cage. Being careful not to disturb the nest, remove as much old shavings and food as possible and replace with new. We use a small plastic spade, designed for a child to use for building sandcastles on the beach. Once you have cleaned the cage, leave the babies to settle for a few minutes before returning the mother to the cage. Putting some treats in the mother's food dish may help to distract her so that she does not become upset about the changes in her cage.

After another two to three days it should be possible to clean the cage completely, including replacing the bedding in the nest. Put the mother in a play box and the babies in a small container. We have found that some mums become very agitated if the babies are put in the play box with her at this early age. The transfer of babies from cage to container and back again will give you a brief chance to handle them. Great care should be taken at this time, as they will normally be very jumpy. Once the cage has been cleaned, put some extra food by the nest and return the babies to the cage. After a few minutes, by which time the babies should have settled down, you can return their mum to the cage. It helps to add a treat to the food dish, to distract mum while the babies explore their clean cage.

21 DAYS ONWARDS

Over the next seven days the babies become quite vocal, usually when minor squabbles occur over a choice morsel of food. If you are able to look into the nest at this stage, you might see two babies having a tug-of-war with a peanut. You may also notice the mother retiring to a corner or shelf to have a quiet period of time away from her offspring. You may also hear her complain occasionally when one of the babies gets overenthusiastic in suckling, forgetting it now has sharp teeth. All of this is quite normal and should not alarm you unduly.

HANDLING

If the mother is amenable, the babies can be handled from 21 days onwards, usually while the mother is playing out of the cage. Once you are able to handle the babies, do so each day, to ensure that the babies are as friendly as possible. Extreme caution should be shown when first handling the babies, as they are very nervous and jumpy. Choose a large surface and handle the babies by holding them no more than a few inches or centimetres above the surface. If any of the babies then jumps or falls – and they usually will – no harm will be done.

SEXING

When you first begin handling the babies, you can determine their sex. Pick up each baby in turn, positioning it so that its back is against the palm of your hand, your thumb is under its chin, and its rear end points towards your little finger. Ensuring that you hold your hand so that the baby's head is uppermost and its rear end is hanging slightly, the genitals should be evident. In the females, the two openings will be very close together, whereas males have a gap with fur between the openings. If you compare baby with baby, the differences will become self-evident.

6. SEPARATING MOTHER AND BABIES

Although the babies will suckle for comfort for a while, from three weeks onwards most of their nourishment comes in the form of solid food. Once the babies are weaned, they should be separated from their mother.
Normally, this can be done around 28 days after birth. However, if the mum looks out of condition, unwell, or seems to be getting very short-tempered with the babies, a day or so earlier would not hurt. The ideal time for separating mum from babies may depend on the number in the litter, the size of the babies, and the mother's state of health. As you become more experienced, you will be better able to judge the right time to separate mum and babies.

We like to take the babies from the mother at 28 days, putting the sexes into separate cages as we go. Generally, it is recognised that Syrian females are receptive at the age of five weeks, but we do not like to take chances, separating females from males by four weeks of age. If you cannot determine the sex of one of the babies, put it in with the males. If it later proves to be a female, you will have one potentially pregnant female, whereas if it is put in with the females and proves to be a male, you may end up with several pregnant females!

RUNNING ON

The minimum age that you should allow the babies to go to their new homes is 28 days. Any earlier and the babies are not well developed enough. Keeping the babies together, in groups of male or female, helps them to overcome the trauma of separation from their mother. It also allows you to check that they are capable of fending for themselves. In the hamster fancy, we use the expression 'running on' when referring to keeping hamsters of the same sex together for a limited time. Running on for a short while has been found to help the babies to grow and to become more self-sufficient.

Running on can cover a period of a few days to a couple of weeks. However, by the age of six weeks – sometimes sooner, sometimes later – each hamster will become increasingly territorial, wanting its own space. As soon as serious squabbles occur, the most aggressive hamster should be given its own cage. Females will normally become territorial earlier than the males.

7. FOSTERING AND HAND-REARING

Hamsters normally make good mothers, but there are occasions when human intervention may be advisable. Should a mother become ill, die, or reject the whole or part of the litter, you will need to consider fostering or hand-rearing the babies if they are to survive.

FOSTERING

Using another female to foster baby hamsters is viable only if the foster mother has had a litter herself, within three to four days of the motherless litter being born. Even then, there is no guarantee of success.

The first decision you make may be heartbreaking, as you consider how many extra babies the foster mum will be able to feed and care for. For example, you cannot introduce 10 extra babies to a mother who already has an equal number of her own. Not only are the chances of any of the fostered babies surviving slim, but such a large number of extra babies may endanger the foster mum's natural babies. Smaller numbers, such as three to four babies in each litter, have a far better chance of survival.

If you have a large number of motherless babies, you will have some very difficult decisions to make. The strongest, biggest and liveliest babies are the most likely to survive, and you may find yourself having no option but to let some of the smaller, weaker babies die. Should you be in the position of having more than one nursing mother to choose from, a few babies with each mother is better than placing all the babies with one foster mother.

The prospective foster mother should be encouraged from her nest and put out to play while the extra babies are added to her own offspring. Some breeders advocate rubbing a little of the soiled shavings from the foster mum's wet corner on each of the newcomers before placing them in the nest. The soiled shavings, carry the foster mother's scent, and, when the babies are rubbed with the shavings, the scent is transferred to them. This may make them more acceptable to the foster mother. However, many other breeders simply place the babies in the nest and let them mingle with the foster mother's own offspring for a few minutes. We have tried both methods and have not been able to say which is best – success seems to depend largely on the temperament of the foster mother.

If the babies have been away from their real mother for some time, they may be a little cold. Put them in a warm place and allow them to warm up before you introduce them to the other babies. The foster mother can then be returned to her cage together with a few choice tidbits put in her food dish. Fortunately, hamsters cannot count (or at least do not seem to), so a small number of extra babies stand a fair chance of being accepted by the foster mother, all other things being equal.

Once the foster babies have been added to the mother's own litter, you should leave mother and babies alone for 12 to 18 hours. Make sure you do not interfere with the nest or distract the mother in any way during this time. If, after 12 to 18 hours, any of the fostered babies have survived, we would consider the fostering a success.

HAND-REARING

Hand-rearing baby hamsters, especially very young ones, is extremely difficult. The older the babies, the more chance they have of survival. Babies of six to seven days have a good chance, whereas newborn babies rarely survive. The success rate is small, but, if there is no alternative and you are willing to try, the rewards (and disappointments) are enormous. Any babies that survive will have a special place in your heart. We know of one case where two teenage boys attempted to raise a litter of six one-day-old babies, and successfully reared one baby. Although initially disappointed to have lost five, the one survivor made everything worthwhile. In our time, we raised many babies from five or six days old and many of these are remembered with special fondness.

One such success story was Mirry (short for Miracle), who was hand-reared from five days. Her mother developed mastitis and had to be taken to the vet, together with her young litter. On our return, the cage was put in a quiet corner for the mother to recover from the trauma of the outing. A few hours later, we checked to see that all was well and discovered that the smallest, weakest baby was missing. After searching the cage and the hamstery floor, we checked the car we had used to take the mother and babies to the vet, and found the baby very cold and apparently lifeless. After a few minutes being hand-warmed, the baby showed some signs of life, so we settled her in a small container placed under a vivarium light. After many setbacks, including pneumonia, she eventually thrived and lived to the grand old age of two years and seven months.

BODY TEMPERATURE

As with all small babies, maintaining body temperature is a problem. If the babies are less than two weeks old, you will need to provide them with an alternative, gentle heat source, which would otherwise have been provided by their mother. The babies will need to be housed in a small container so that heat can be concentrated in a small area. A 2-litre (4-US-pint/3.5-UK-pint) ice cream container, or something similar, is ideal. Put a thin layer of shavings on the bottom of the container, make a nest out of paper bedding, and add the bedding to the container.

You can provide a heat source in a number of ways. Placing the container on a hot water bottle wrapped in a towel works very well, as does a very warm airing cupboard. Alternatively, you could use an infrared lamp suspended above the container, a vivarium light suspended above the container, or a low-watt (15w) light bulb. If you use an infrared heat lamp you must take great care to position the lamp at the correct height above the container – too close may lead to overheating.

FEEDING

Babies less than seven days old will need feeding at two-hourly intervals. They will also need to have their tummies rubbed to stimulate the passage of waste. Although full-cream cow's milk can be used, we have had more success with commercially packed kitten milk, slightly warmed. A twist of muslin or slim cloth poked into the end of an eyedropper will act as a teat, and, as the hamsters grow, they will learn to drink from the end of a teaspoon. Initially, the babies will take only one drop of milk at a time, but their consumption of milk will increase as they grow. We have found that, after giving milk, it is advisable to give each baby a drop or two of tepid boiled water. This helps to combat any stickiness left by the milk.

HAMSTER COLOURS

From the original golden colour of the wild hamster, breeders
have developed a plethora of different colours and varieties.

Golden – the original ▶
coat colour.

A Yellow Syrian
◀ showing the black
ticking on the end
of the hair.

A Yellow Satin
Syrian – note the
sheen that is ▶
characteristic of
the Satin coat.

HAMSTER COLOURS

A Golden Band. The band on this hamster ◀ is broken and narrow so this animal may not do well in a show.

Dark Grey Band. Ideally, the band of white should be ▶ one-third of the body length for showing purposes.

Longhaired Mink. ◀ Note the red eyes and pale ears.

HAMSTER COLOURS

Chocolate – one of ▶
the newer colours.

Dove Dominant Spot.
In show-quality
◀ hamsters there should
be far more spotting
all over.

Longhaired Sable.
Note the characteristic ▶
light-coloured eye
rings (spectacles).

HAMSTER COLOURS

Black Tortoiseshell and White, showing ◀ the three distinct colours of black, yellow and white.

Black Tortoiseshell and White Dominant Spot. Ideally, for showing, ▶ this hamster should have an equal spread of all three colours.

Black Banded – an ◀ arresting colour combination.

HAMSTER COLOURS

Although normally referred to as an Albino, genetically this hamster is a Flesh ▶ Eared White. Albino has yet to be isolated in the hamster.

Black Eyed Cream – one of the most easily available ◀ colours. This hamster is young and the colour should deepen with age.

Longhaired Black Eyed Ivory – not a ▶ commonly found colour.

LONGHAIRED VARIETIES

Longhaired hamsters are a popular choice – but profuse coats require regular care to keep clean and tangle-free.

Longhaired Black Eyed Cream (left) and a longhaired Mink Roan female (right) – the coat is much more profuse in males.

Longhaired Sable male: note the lighter base colour showing through the longer hair.

Dark Grey: note the clarity of the flashes.

DWARF BREEDS

The Dwarf breeds are often more sociable with each other, but they are not always so easy to handle – plus they are particularly good at escaping!

Dominant Spot Chinese hamster – the extended hind part shows this hamster is definitely male.

Pair of Roborovski hamsters – it is unusual to see these hamsters still!

Normal Campbell Russian – the natural wild colour.

Platinum Campbell Russian – one of the newer colour variations.

WINTER WHITE

A pair of Winter White Normal ◄ hamsters (the original wild colour).

Sapphire Winter White – the coat has a much ► lighter appearance than the Normal (above).

Winter White Pearl – this colour variation ◄ resembles the winter coat of Winter Whites living in the wild.

After feeding, you will need to rub each hamster's tummy to stimulate waste production. Gently move a finger up and down the tummy area and wipe away the waste with a piece of kitchen roll or cotton wool (cotton). You should also clean and dry the hamsters' mouths before returning each baby to the nest. When the hamsters are between 7 and 14 days old, you can gradually increase the interval between feeds from two hours to five. Once you have established this new feeding routine, you can move on to regular feeds three times a day, with the last very late at night. Solid foods – such as runny porridge made with milk, or liquid baby foods – should be introduced in the same way you would introduce them to a litter with a mother (see page 117).

HAND-REARING RUNTS
Occasionally, a runt (i.e. a very small baby) appears in a litter. Without intervention, the runt would probably die, much as nature and natural selection intend. However, we have found that runts of various litters are usually strong fighters, and we try our hardest to help them survive. This sometimes means that we go against our own advice of not interfering with babies at an early age. For example, from the age of seven days, we help the runt of the litter by offering runny porridge from the end of a teaspoon while mum is enjoying a run in her play box.

With special care, the runt of a litter can grow to normal size and lead a healthy, happy and normal existence. A well-cared-for runt will quickly catch up with its siblings, and, contrary to popular belief, the smallest of the litter is not necessarily the weakest or the most timid. It is not unusual for the runt to start 'bullying' its larger siblings. We once took the runts from a very large litter that was not thriving, and placed them with a slightly older litter containing a smaller number of babies. When squabbling was heard at three weeks, we investigated, dreading what we would find. When we looked in the cage, however, we saw one of the runts picking on his bigger (and older) foster brothers and sisters. As he was a longhaired Yellow, and all our Yellows have names beginning with the letter Y, he then became known as "Yangster, the little gangster!" At the time of going to print, he has just celebrated his second birthday, and in no way would anyone guess, by looking at his size now, that he had once been a runt.

8. RECORD KEEPING
If you intend to breed more than the occasional litter, record keeping is a must. This will entail naming, or at least numbering, your hamsters so that accurate records (pedigrees) can be kept. Your records will help you to choose
pairings for a particular colour, will help ensure that you are not inbreeding, and will help to determine whether your hamsters are the right age for breeding.

Your records do not need to be vastly complicated. Each hamster should have its own record, stating the hamster's name (or number), date of birth, colour, parents (if known), and where purchased (if applicable). You can record these details in a notebook, or you could use small index or record cards. You will need a card for each hamster, with the cards filed either in alphabetical order, or by date of birth. If you have a computer, a simple database can be designed to record these details. Over the years our records have gone through all these stages, and, in the last few years, with the advent of computer programmes specialising in recording animal (and human) family trees, we have transferred all our records to one of these programs. However, we still retain a copy of our records on index cards for quick reference in the hamstery, and, most importantly, in case of a major computer malfunction, a permanent record would still be available.

The more information you have in your records, the more useful they will be. You should make a note of each mating, the date of birth of the litter, the size and content of the litter (including the sex and colour of each baby), on each of the parent's record cards. If you buy a hamster to mate with one you already own, try to obtain as much information about its parents as possible. If you are planning to breed a single litter only, you should still record the date of birth so that you know how old your babies are. Many people assume that it is easy to remember the date of birth of a single litter, but it is surprisingly easy to become confused and miscalculate the babies' ages by as much as one week. A week may not seem like much, but an underestimation of a week can result in unwanted pregnancies, while an overestimation may lead to the babies being weaned and rehomed far too early.

9. COLOURS AND PATTERNS

In this section the colours and patterns are described in general terms, to give the reader an idea of what the hamster looks like. If you are going to exhibit your hamster and join one of the many hamster clubs around the world, you will be given a list of Standards, to which your hamster should conform. Each colour has a different Standard, and, unfortunately, the Standards differ slightly between different clubs and different countries. Furthermore, some of the colours described here have not, at time of writing, been accepted as a Standard colour, although they are fairly common. Conversely, some of the accepted Standard colours may now be quite rare. The descriptions given here are very general; they are not intended to replace the Standards laid out by each individual club. If you intend to show your hamster, you will need to join a club and ask for the club's official Standards.

Do not be overly surprised if your hamster does not quite match any of the colours described below. Slight variations can be found in all colours. For example, colours that include the Umbrous gene (see below) may vary enormously. In addition, there are 'mongrel' colours, which do not match any of the described colours. Our first hamster, Gorgeous, was one such hamster. Although she won many Non-Standard classes at hamster shows, no one could manage to assign a particular colour to her.

Where applicable, each colour below is described with its genotype (i.e. the genetic constitution responsible for its colour) given in brackets. For more information on genotypes and breeding for specific colours, see the sections on genetics and colour combinations later in this chapter.

Wherever possible, we have given the date when a colour first appeared. Often, dates are not recorded when colours travel from one country to another, especially if there are no official clubs to keep records. In the case of some of the lesser-known colours, it is impossible to be sure how many countries now have that colour available.

TERMINOLOGY

To help you to follow the colour descriptions, there first follows a brief explanation of the terminology used:

- **Ticking:** the endmost tip of each individual hair is a contrasting colour to the rest. Ticking is not present in all hamsters.
- **Topcoat:** the fur between the tip of the hair and the base colour of the hair, i.e. the middle of the hair. In a hamster that has no ticking, the tip and the topcoat are the same colour.
- **Base colour:** the bottom part of each individual hair (i.e. the part nearest the skin) is a different colour from the rest. Not all hamsters have a base colour – some hamsters' fur is the same colour from root to tip, but, if a base colour is present, it can be seen by blowing gently on the topcoat to part it.
- **Belly fur:** the fur covering the underside of the hamster, between its four legs.
- **Cheek flashings:** markings on either side of the face.
- **Crescents:** lighter markings on either side of the cheek flashings.
- **Chest band:** a thin band of colour around the chest (just in front of the front legs).
- **Self coloured:** an animal that is the same colour all over. However, some self-coloured hamsters may have a small white line under the chin, a small spot of white on the tummy, and four socks, i.e. an area just above each foot that is white. Socks are more prominent on darker self-coloured animals.
- **Agouti:** a colour that normally has ticking, cheek flashes, and crescents.

COLOURS AND PATTERNS
See also page 139: Simple Genetics.

GOLDEN
This is the original colour of the wild Syrian hamster. During the first years of exhibiting, selective breeding developed different shades of this colour. These shades formed the basis of the different classes of hamsters at early hamster shows. Unfortunately, the introduction of many new colours over the years has meant that some of these shades are very rarely seen.

DARK GOLDEN (++ WILD-TYPE AGOUTI)
The rich, dark-mahogany-red topcoat with a dark-grey under colour and heavy black ticking gives this hamster a very impressive appearance. There is usually a heavy concentration of black ticking on the top of the head and around the eyes. The belly fur is ivory, with a grey under colour, and the chest band is a rich mahogany. The cheek flashes are black, bordered on each side with pale ivory crescents. The eyes are black and the ears are a very dark grey that is almost black.

NORMAL GOLDEN (++ WILD-TYPE AGOUTI)
This hamster is bright chestnut in colour, lightly and evenly ticked with mahogany and a slate-grey base colour. It has dark-grey (almost black) cheek flashes, with ivory crescents. The belly fur is also ivory with a bright-chestnut chest band. The ears are very dark grey and the eyes are black. Frequently, a bad example of a Dark Golden is mistaken for this colour.

LIGHT GOLDEN (++ WILD-TYPE AGOUTI)
The topcoat of this hamster is a light, fawn-coloured gold, with a slate-grey base colour but no ticking. The crescents are ivory (almost white), bordering dark-grey

(almost black) cheek flashings. The chest band is also a light fawn-coloured gold, while the belly fur is ivory (almost white). The ears are grey and the eyes are black. This colour is now very rarely seen on the show bench.

SEPIA

This colour was developed in 1961 by selective breeding of Golden hamsters, but today it has become another of the endangered colours. The Sepia has a light, tawny beige topcoat with very dark (almost black), even ticking, and a base colour of pale grey. The cheek flashes are almost black, with ivory (almost white) crescents, and the belly fur is ivory (almost white), with a chest band of light, tawny beige. The eyes are black and ears are dark grey.

BEIGE (bbdgdg)

Discovered in 1964, Beige is a colour that has virtually disappeared from the hamster show bench. The topcoat is a soft, pale grey, with a brown-coloured tone lightly and evenly ticked with dark beige/brown. Beneath the topcoat the base colour is slate grey. White crescents surround the dark-beige/brown cheek flashes, and a dark-beige/brown chest band decorates the ivory-coloured belly fur. The eyes are very dark brown (almost black) and the ears are very dark beige.

BLACK (aa)

Black made its first appearance about 1985, and in the short time it has existed it has made a huge impact by producing many new colours. The ideal for this colour is totally black, but, at present, small patches of white can be found under the chin and the chest, while the white above the feet is very evident. Hopefully, with selective breeding over time, it may be possible to lose these white patches. A Black hamster will also have black eyes and ears. It is now becoming easier to obtain this colour, at least in Europe.

BLONDE (Lglgpp)

This colour seems to have emerged in the mid 1960s. When we first started exhibiting in the late 1980s it was still found on the show bench, but since then it seems to have gone out of favour. In recent years, it is rarely seen at all.

A Blonde hamster is a creamy-blonde colour with a light-grey base coat. Light-grey cheek flashes are bordered with ivory crescents. The ivory belly fur has a creamy-blonde, orange-tinged chest band, and the muzzle tends to be orange-tinted as well. The eyes are claret red and the ears are grey.

CHOCOLATE (SABLE) (UUeebb)

First making an appearance in the 1970s, this hamster has a mid-chocolate-brown coat with black eyes and brown ears. This colour is still not very widespread, but numbers are increasing.

CHOCOLATE (BLACK) (aabb)

Appearing in the UK in the mid 1990s, this colour offers an alternative to the original (sable) Chocolate. It is a dark-chocolate-brown hamster with black eyes and brown ears. This colour is now fairly sought after, so numbers are increasing gradually.

CINNAMON (pp)

First seen in 1958, today the Cinnamon is one of the most commonly kept colours. During our early years of keeping hamsters, this colour dominated our hamstery. The topcoat is a rich orange, while the base colour is slate grey. The cheek flashes are brown and the crescents ivory. The creamy ivory belly fur has a blue base colour and a rich russet-brown chest band. The eyes are bright claret and the ears flesh-brown. Many pet owners frequently mistake this colour for a Golden hamster.

CINNAMON FAWN (ppruru)

The Cinnamon Fawn is a very rare colour. It is first mentioned in 1961, in the results sheets of the Midlands Hamster Club. It has a pastel-orange topcoat with a light-grey base colour and pale-grey cheek flashes bordered by white crescents. The belly fur is white with a pastel-orange chest band. Ruby eyes are complemented by flesh-coloured ears.

COPPER (UUeebbpp)

This is another colour that appeared in the late 1970s and has become increasingly sought after. A recent revival of this colour has resulted in numbers steadily increasing of late. The Copper hamster is a rich, copper colour all over, with garnet-coloured eyes and copper-grey ears.

CREAM (BLACK EYED) (ee)

This was one of the first colour mutations, appearing around 1951. Today, the Black Eyed Cream is one of the most commonly found colours. This self-coloured hamster is a deep, rich, cream/sandy colour all over, with black eyes and dark-grey ears.

CREAM (RED EYED) (eepp)

The Red Eyed Cream first appeared in 1961. Today, it remains very popular, being a colour frequently seen for sale. The Red Eyed Cream hamster is a peach colour all over with claret-red eyes and peach-grey ears. In the early years, there was strong opposition against giving this colour a UK Standard, and it was not until the late 1980s that the colour gained acceptance. The US hamster fancy based their Standard on the UK model.

CREAM (RUBY EYED) (eeruru)

This colour was first seen in 1948, but is now very rare. It has been many years since this colour has been seen in the UK and the US. We have heard of one or two being reported, but it will take much time and effort before this colour makes its appearance back in hamster shows, if it happens at all.

The Ruby Eyed Cream has a warm pastel-cream coat with ruby eyes and flesh-coloured ears. The male is supposedly sterile after approximately 12 weeks of age, which makes it very difficult to breed this colour successfully.

DOVE (aapp)

As this colour has some of the genes for Black in its make-up, we suspect it first appeared in the late 1980s. Dove is a most sought-after colour, and demand has led to increasing numbers being available, although mainly at hamster shows. It is a pretty colour; soft, greyish brown with red eyes and flesh-coloured ears.

GREY (DARK) (dgdg)

Discovered in 1964, this colour is still loved by the pet-owning public and by hamster fanciers. Its pearly-grey topcoat has a dark, slate-grey base colour and heavy black ticking. The cheek flashes are black with ivory-coloured crescents. The belly fur is also ivory with a grey base coat, while the chest band is a very dark slate grey. The eyes are black with a black ring of fur around them, and the ears are an almost-black dark grey.

GREY (LIGHT) (Lglg)

First seen in 1965, this colour is far less common in recent times, with very few animals appearing in shows. The topcoat is a buttermilk colour, complemented by a dark, slate-coloured base colour, heavily and evenly ticked with dark grey. It has almost-black cheek flashes bordered by buttermilk crescents. The belly fur is also buttermilk with a grey under colour, and the chest band is dark brown/grey. The eyes are black and the ears are dark grey.

GREY (SILVER) (SgSg)

This is a relatively recent colour development, which first appeared around 1985. We must admit to having a very soft spot for this colour, because, in general, Silver Grey hamsters always have a great temperament, making ideal pets.

Overall, the Silver Grey is a chinchilla colour. The light silver-grey topcoat, heavily ticked with black, has an underlying base colour of dark slate grey. The cheek flashes are black with silver crescents. The belly fur is also a light silver grey with a mid-grey chest band. The eyes are black and the ears are very dark, appearing almost black.

HONEY (Male: ppTo; Female: ppToTo)

Honey began to appear sometime after 1962, and has become very popular among pet owners and the hamster fancy alike. It is a fairly common colour, with a light cinnamon-orange topcoat with no ticking, cinnamon cheek flashes, and ivory (almost white) crescents. The belly fur is also ivory (almost white) and the chest band is a light cinnamon-orange colour. It has claret-red eyes and flesh-grey ears.

IVORY (BLACK EYED) (eeLglg or eedgdg)

Like the Blonde, the Black Eyed Ivory is thought to have appeared in the mid 1960s but is very rarely seen today. It is a pale greyish-cream hamster with black eyes and dark-grey ears.

IVORY (RED EYED) (eeLglgpp or eedgdgpp)

The history and fate of the Red Eyed Ivory is, unfortunately, the same as the Blonde and Black Eyed Ivory – this is another colour that was once very popular among the hamster fancy but now makes very rare appearances. This hamster resembles the Black Eyed Ivory, with the exception of its garnet-coloured eyes and its pink-grey ears.

LILAC (dgdgpp)

This colour was developed in the 1960s, making its appearance at hamster shows in the middle of that decade. It remains a sought-after colour at hamster shows, and a small number have found their way into the pet market.

The Lilac hamster has a soft, pale-grey topcoat with a pink tinge, and a base colour of soft, pale grey. Ivory crescents, claret-red eyes, and pink-grey ears accentuate the warm-grey cheek flashes. Unfortunately, the pink tinge has been replaced with a brown tinge in recent years, but we are desperately trying to breed back to the original colour that is liked so much.

LILAC PEARL (Male: dgdgppTo; Female: dgdgppToTo)
Discovered in 1988, this colour has never been particularly popular. Today it is rarely seen, due to the low numbers of Lilacs and Smoke Pearls needed for its make-up. It has a pale pinkish-grey topcoat, lightly ticked with grey. The cheeks flashes are pale grey with pale-ivory crescents. The belly fur is also pale ivory with a pale pinkish-grey chest band. The eyes are red and it has flesh-coloured ears.

MELANISTIC YELLOW (Male: aaTo; Female: aaToTo)
This colour first made its appearance in the UK in the mid 1990s, and has subsequently spread to many other countries. The topcoat is a rich, dusky yellow tipped with black. The eyes are black and the ears dark grey. This can be a very striking hamster, especially in the longhaired variety, because, when the hamster moves, glimpses of the yellow colour can be seen through the black.

MINK (UUeepp)
Unfortunately, it is not known when this colour first appeared, but we suspect it was sometime in the late 1970s. It is an orange-brown hamster with dark-red eyes and very pale-brown ears. The Mink is not the most common of colours, but it can be found at some hamster shows and seems to be growing in popularity.

MINK (BLUE) (UUeedgdgpp)
As with the Mink, the history of this colour is unknown. The Blue Mink has a deep-brown coat with a bluish tinge all over. It has garnet-red eyes and very pale-brown eyes. Good specimens of this colour can be very hard to find.

MOSAIC
Although references were made to this colour mutation in the early 1950s, not until 1955 did this colour really start to make an appearance. They can still be found today, but as a rarity.

The Mosaic hamster resembles a normal-coloured hamster (usually the Black Eyed Cream), but it has a patch of black hair appearing somewhere on its body, which varies in size from a single hair to the size of a fingernail.

RUBY EYED FAWN (ruru)
The UK Standard for this colour was set in 1955. Vague references were made in the National Hamster Council Journals during the preceding year, but nothing was formalised until 1955. This colour is extremely rare and may no longer exist. There is no documentation to suggest that the original colour spread beyond Europe.

The Ruby Eyed Fawn has a clear, bright-fawn topcoat with a light, slate-grey under colour. Fawn cheek flashes and ivory-coloured (almost white) crescents complement the ivory (almost white) belly fur and fawn chest band, while the ruby-red eyes and pale-grey ears provide a striking contrast.

RUST (bb)

Discovered in 1961, Rust is often mistaken for Cinnamon. The topcoat is a rich orange-brown, lightly and evenly ticked with brown and a base colour of brownish grey. The cheek flashes are a deep rust-brown colour, surrounded by ivory crescents. The ivory belly fur has a pale-grey base colour and a deep rust-brown chest band. The eyes are a very dark brown, which is almost black, while the ears are dark grey with a hint of pink.

Although Rust has existed for more than 40 years, it is not a common colour. Unfortunately, the continuation of this colour has been left to a few dedicated breeders, making this hamster something of a rarity.

SABLE (UUee)

This colour was the original 'Black' when it was discovered in 1975. The name was changed to Sable when the Melanistic Black was introduced. The topcoat is almost black with an ivory cream base coat. The belly fur is also black and it has black eyes and dark-grey ears. Circles of cream/ivory can be found around the eyes, which gives the hamster the appearance of wearing spectacles. It is not unusual for the fur to gain an orange tinge as the hamster ages. Longhaired males can look very striking with their long fur being orange at the end, turning cream towards the middle, deepening to an almost black colour, and then fading to cream at the roots.

SILVER AGOUTI

This is a white animal with a silvery base colour. It is thought to have emerged at the same time as the Silver Sable, in the middle 1990s.

SILVER SABLE (UueeSgsg)

This colour made its UK appearance in the mid 1990s, and has subsequently spread to other countries. The topcoat is almost black with a silvery base colour, complemented by the dark-grey ears and the black belly fur. The eyes are also black, surrounded by ivory-coloured circles, which, like the Sable, give it the appearance of wearing spectacles.

SMOKE PEARL (Male: dgdgToô; Female: dgdgToTo)

First appearing in 1971, this colour has gained in favour over last few years due to its highly attractive appearance. However, despite its rise in popularity, this hamster can be seen and bought only at hamster shows.

The Smoke Pearl has a pale-grey coat with heavy black ticking, and black cheek flashes bordered by ivory crescents. It has ivory belly fur with a rich dusky-yellow chest band. The eyes are black and the ears are dark grey.

WHITE (BLACK EYED) (eeDsds or eeWhwh)

Mention of this colour is made as early as 1961, when specimens were exhibited in a Midland Hamster Club Show in the UK. Since that time, the colour has spread to many other countries. This is a totally white animal with black eyes and flesh-coloured ears.

WHITE (DARK EARED) (cdcd)

This colour first appeared in 1952, and today can be easily found in pet shops and on the show bench at hamster shows. This pure-white hamster has dark-grey, almost-black ears, and red eyes that darken with age.

WHITE (FLESH EARED) *(cdcdpp)*

This hamster is also known as the Albino or the Pale Eared Albino, but it is not a true Albino. It is first mentioned in the National Hamster Council Journal of 1956, and, although the colour is not popular among pet owners, many are found on the show benches at hamster shows. As its name suggests, this hamster is white all over with pink eyes and flesh-coloured ears.

YELLOW (Male: To; Female: ToTo)

First discovered in 1962, today this colour is very common. The topcoat is a rich dusky yellow, with heavy, even black ticking and a base coat of ivory yellow. The cheek flashes are black with ivory crescents, while the belly fur is ivory with a rich dusky-yellow chest band. The eyes are black and the ears an almost-black dark grey.

Increasingly, a paler Yellow (known as the Ghost Yellow) is making its appearance on the show benches. This is a pale-yellow hamster with hardly any ticking. If entered into the Straight Class at a hamster show, the Ghost Yellow would be heavily penalised by a judge, as it is not a true Yellow.

TORTOISESHELL

In 1962, the National Hamster Council Journal refers to a hamster described as a mix between a Golden and a Honey. Today, this hamster is known as the Tortoiseshell. This bi-coloured animal has patches of yellow mixed with its basic colour, e.g. Golden, Dark Grey, Cinnamon, or Black, etc. The shade of yellow will vary depending on the base colour. The amount of yellow on the hamster will vary, but the ideal is equal amounts of each colour. The Tortoiseshell colour gene is sex-linked, so all Tortoiseshell hamsters are female.

TORTOISESHELL AND WHITE

In 1963, the National Hamster Council Journal describes hamsters that resemble a mix between the Golden and Honey bands. Today, this is a tri-coloured animal with patches of white and yellow mixed with another basic colour. As with the bi-coloured Tortoiseshell the shade of yellow will vary depending on the base colour. The ratio of the three colours can also vary, although the ideal is equal amounts of all three, spread evenly over the hamster's body. Once again, the Tortoiseshell gene in this hamster's genetic make-up means that all Tortoiseshell and White hamsters are female.

UMBROUS

First occurring in 1975, this particular colour gene enabled many new colours to be generated, including Sable, Mink, Copper and Caramel.

BANDS

The first bands were reported in 1957. They are hamsters that have a white band around their middle. The width of the band may vary, from a narrow strip of white to a wide expanse that leaves just the head and the rump coloured. For exhibition purposes, the band should be about a third of the body length.

PIEBALD

The Piebald hamster was first recorded in 1945. It is a coloured hamster with white spots, varying from one or two small spots to huge areas of white that make the hamster appear totally white. Patches of colour may also appear on the belly. Where coloured fur and white fur meet, there is always some brindling.

This particular pattern is very hard to breed. When the Dominant Spot began to appear, which is easier to breed, the Piebald variety became far fewer in number and today it is very unlikely that you will find one.

DOMINANT SPOT

In 1964, the Dominant Spot patterning appeared, and quickly superseded the Piebald. The Dominant Spot is a coloured hamster with white spots and white belly fur. The spots vary from one or two small spots to huge areas of white, and both the UK and the US Standards describe this hamster as "a white animal with coloured spots". If you intend to exhibit Dominant Spots, the spotting should be evenly distributed.

WHITE BELLIED

In 1958, some White Bellied Golden hamsters were exported from the US to the UK. While the White Bellied gene can be present in all colours, the presence of white belly fur does not necessarily mean that the hamster carries the White Bellied Gene. For example, Dominant Spots and Bands already have white belly fur, and it is very difficult to distinguish them from animals with the White Bellied gene. Self-coloured animals with the gene are generally Roans, but in Agouti colours the gene will turn the belly fur white.

ROAN

Roan patterning gives the appearance of a white hamster with coloured ticking, the ticking usually being heavier on the head and decreasing towards the tail. The White Bellied gene causes this patterning, so care should be taken when trying to produce this colour.

COAT TYPES

REX COATED

In 1970, the first Rex coated hamsters were recorded. The easiest way to discover if your hamster is Rex coated is to look at the whiskers – Rex hamsters have curly whiskers instead of the normal straight ones.

The coat is also curly but will vary from hamster to hamster. For example, longhaired hamsters may have wavy fur (as well as looking in constant need of grooming) instead of curls. One minor problem associated with the Rex is Entropion, i.e. an inward-turning eyelid that results in irritation of the eyeball (see page 93).

SATIN

First appearing in 1968, this coat type makes the fur very fine and gives it a satin sheen. If the fur is stroked the wrong way, the colour will appear to change, similar to stroking velvet the wrong way.

LONGHAIRED
The first longhaired hamsters appeared in 1972. With careful breeding, housing and grooming, the hair can reach 4 inches (10 cms) in length on the male.

10. SIMPLE GENETICS

Part of the appeal of breeding hamsters, apart from watching the babies grow, is waiting and watching to see what colours the babies will be. Theoretically, you can predict the results, if the backgrounds of the parents are known. However, what is predicted and what is produced can be two different matters.

Understanding some of the terms used in genetics helps to unravel the mysteries of breeding for colour. When we first started exhibiting and breeding, we were confused by the technical terms (e.g. dominant, recessive, compatible, etc.) used with such ease by more experienced breeders. To avoid such confusion here, we have provided a short explanation for each of these terms.

GENETIC TERMS

DOMINANT
This is a term used for a genetic trait that is visible on the animal. It would be impossible for a characteristic (e.g. a Band) to appear in a litter unless it is visible on one of the parents. For example, if the parents have no visible spots, then none of the offspring will have spots. Similarly, if neither of the parents has a Satin coat, none of the offspring will have it.

LETHAL DOMINANT
Light Grey and Dominant Spot are classed as Lethal Dominant genes. Offspring that inherit two doses of the Lethal Dominant gene – one from the mother, one from the father – would die in the womb.

Two Light Grey (Lglg) hamsters mated together would result in a litter with the following genetic make-up:

	Lg	lg
Lg	LgLg	lglg
lg	Lglg	Lglg

Translated, this means that 50 per cent of the offspring will be Light Grey (Lglg), 25 per cent will be Golden (lglg), and 25 per cent will be Light Grey (LgLg) babies that die in the womb (Homozygote).

A similar result would occur if two Dominant Spots were mated, i.e. approximately 25 per cent of the litter would die in the womb as a result of inheriting two doses of the Lethal Dominant Dominant Spot gene.

SEMI-LETHAL DOMINANT
This gene is very similar to the Lethal Dominant except that the babies that inherit the two doses (Homozygote) do not die in the womb but are born deformed. The White Bellied gene is a Semi-lethal Dominant gene.

139

RECESSIVE

Recessive genes are the opposite of Dominant genes. This means that they may not be visible on the animal, but they will still be carried in the hamster's cells. However, should two hamsters with compatible recessive genes be bred together, some of the offspring (known as First Generation Offspring or F1 for short) may have a different coat colour or type. For example, two shorthaired Syrians may produce some longhaired offspring if both parents carry the recessive longhaired gene. Recessive colour genes work in the same manner: two Cinnamons mated together may produce some Lilac babies, if both Cinnamons have Lilac in their backgrounds (albeit many generations previously).

COMPATIBLE COLOURS

This term refers to colours that are compatible, i.e. both hamsters in a chosen mating pair share the same colour, or have colour genes that share a common genotype, so that offspring of a desired colour are produced. For example, Cinnamon (pp) mated to Lilac (dgdgpp) would produce a litter of Cinnamons, because the colours are compatible or share a common genotype. Two hamsters of the same colour mated together would normally produce F1 offspring of that colour unless both parents were carrying the same recessive gene of another colour, in which case some of the litter may be of the recessive gene colour.

NON-COMPATIBLE COLOURS

Two hamsters of non-compatible colours will produce offspring that 'revert' to the original colour of Golden because the parents did not share a common genotype for colour. However, the F1 offspring will still carry the colour genes of both parents, so if one F1 hamster is mated to another, some of their progeny (known as Second Generation or F2) will be the same colour as one of the grandparents. For example, if a Dark Grey (dgdg) is mated to a Black Eyed Cream (ee), the F1 offspring will all be Golden (EeDgdg). If two of these are then mated, the resulting F2 offspring will consist of nine Golden, three Black Eyed Creams (ee), three Dark Greys (dgdg) and one Black Eyed Ivory (eedgdg), as demonstrated in this table.

	EDg	eDg	Edg	edg
EDg	EEDgDg (1)	EeDgDg (1)	EEDgdg (1)	EeDgdg (1)
eDg	EeDgDg (1)	eeDgDg (2)	EeDgdg (1)	eeDgdg (2)
Edg	EEDgdg (1)	EeDgdg (1)	EEdgdg (3)	Eedgdg (3)
edg	EeDgdg (1)	eeDgdg (2)	Eedgdg (3)	eedgdg (4)

(1) = Golden
(2) = Black Eyed Cream
(3) = Dark Grey
(4) = Black Eyed Ivory

STRAIGHT/PURE

This term usually means that the parents, grandparents, and great grandparents, etc., of a hamster were the same colour. Where records have been kept for many years, a breeder may be able to say that a colour has been 'straight' for five or more generations. Hamsters that have been bred straight for many generations are far less likely to produce offspring of different colour.

SPLIT

This term was used extensively in our early days of exhibiting, but is used less frequently of late. Straight Golden mated to Straight Cinnamon would produce Goldens 'split' for Cinnamon. In other words, the offspring will appear Golden but will carry the gene for Cinammon, which, in turn, can be passed on to their own young.

CARRIERS

A carrier is a hamster that carries a colour gene that has been inherited from an ancestor but one that is not visible by looking at the hamster. Carriers can be found by studying the hamster's pedigree. Some colours are not readily available and carriers can provide an alternative to someone looking to breed for a rarer colour. When we were looking for Dark Grey stock and were unable to find any, we settled for Goldens with a Dark Grey parent. When the Goldens were mated to the Dark Greys some Dark Grey babies were produced.

INBREEDING

Inbreeding is the practice of mating closely related hamsters to one another. In the hamster fancy, inbreeding is used for certain purposes only. For example, if a 'new' colour emerged in a litter, a brother/sister, mother/son, father/daughter mating could be tried to obtain a nucleus of animals of the new colour, or to breed carriers of the new colour genotype. Continued inbreeding can result in a lowering of fertility in males, and a general loss of size and vigour, with each generation getting smaller and less robust. Inbreeding can allow good points to flourish, but any weaknesses in the line would be accentuated, so inbreeding is normally avoided where possible.

RATIO

In genetics, the term ratio refers to the mix of colours, hair type and sex in a litter. The ratio is the mix of these attributes that can be expected from a mathematical calculation. In reality, of course, nature does not always follow mathematical formulae, but, if the ratio is taken over a number of litters (e.g. 10 to 20), nature's results coincide with what is expected mathematically. This can be clearly seen when sexing a litter. Mathematically, the litter should have a ratio of 1:1 (50 per cent of each sex). Very often, an individual litter has a large majority of one sex, but if the number of males and females is totalled over 10 litters, it normally works out at 50 per cent of each sex. Over the years, we have found that spring litters seem to have more females, while autumn litters have more males, but, if the average is taken over a full year, the ratio of male to female is 1:1.

Mating a Banded hamster to a non-patterned hamster should produce 50 per cent with Bands and 50 per cent without Bands. Many people, especially if relatively new to hamster breeding, are sometimes disappointed that the Banded young have not inherited the perfect Band of the parent. Unfortunately, while the gene follows the rule of inheritance, the formation of the Band is random. Some hamsters with unprepossessing Bands will produce young with well-formed Bands, while another with a perfect Band will produce young with poor or broken Bands.

The same applies to the Dominant Spot gene. The spotting can range from one or two spots of white on a coloured hamster, to one that is white with just a few spots of colour. The one characteristic frequently seen on one of these spotted hamsters is a blaze of white on the forehead.

The breeding of Roans also follows that of the Band and Dominant Spot, with the litter expected to contain some Roan hamsters and some plain hamsters. The Roaning can be haphazard, with some hamsters better marked than others.

Breeding patterned animals, especially if you wish to exhibit them, can be highly frustrating but it is always interesting, and when a well-patterned hamster eventually appears, the satisfaction is enormous.

WHITE BELLIED GENE (ANOPHTHALMIC)

The principle governing inheritance of the White Bellied gene is one that must be understood by anyone considering breeding hamsters. It is a Semi-Lethal Dominant gene, and hamsters with the White Bellied gene always have white belly fur. Unfortunately, to complicate the matter further, not all hamsters with white belly fur have the gene. The problem with mating two hamsters carrying this gene is that the resultant litter will contain 25 per cent normal hamsters, 50 per cent White Bellied hamsters, and 25 per cent Anophthalmic Whites, as seen in the following table.

	Wh	wh
Wh	WhWh (3)	Whwh (2)
wh	Whwh (2)	whwh (1)

(1) = Normal
(2) = White Bellied
(3) = Anophthalmic Whites.

Another name for Anophthalmic Whites is Eyeless Whites, which, as the name suggests, is a White hamster with no eyes, or, if the eyes are present, they are rudimentary.

Mating a hamster with the White Bellied gene to one that does not have the gene will result in a litter comprising 50 per cent normal and 50 per cent White Bellied. This seems straightforward until you come to breeding patterned hamsters, such as Bands, Spots and Roans, all of which have white belly fur. All Roan hamsters carry the White Bellied gene (it is this gene that causes the mottling effect of a Roan) so a Roan should never be mated to a White Bellied hamster. However, it is impossible to tell by looking at the belly fur of Bands and Spots, which, if any, has the White Bellied gene. Despite our experience in breeding hamsters we do not mate Band to Band or Spot to Spot.

SEX-LINKED COLOUR GENES

All Tortoiseshell hamsters are female, as are all Tortoiseshell cats. The expected number of Tortoiseshells in a litter produced by a Tortoiseshell female mated with a normal male would not be high. For example, if a Tortoiseshell female is mated to a Yellow male the litter should comprise 25 per cent Yellow males, 25 per cent Golden males, 25 per cent Yellow females, and 25 per cent Tortoiseshell females.

To understand why Tortoiseshell hamsters are always female, we need to further investigate the genetics of the Yellow gene. Yellow is a co-dominant gene, which means that it shows when present but it can exist alongside another colour. Yellow males have the genotype To, while Yellow females have the genotype ToTo. This is because the Yellow gene is carried on the X (female) chromosome. Females have two X chromosomes, and males have one X chromosome and one Y (male) chromosome.

As females have two X chromosomes, their genotype can be ToTo (Yellow), toto (Non-Yellow) or Toto (Tortoiseshell). As males have only one X chromosome, they will always be Yellow (To_) or Non-Yellow (to_). This is a very simple explanation of a fairly complicated gene.

One way to increase the chances of producing Tortoiseshell hamsters is to mate a 'straight' Yellow male to a 'straight' Non-Yellow female. This mating will ensure that all the females in the litter are Tortoiseshell.

11. COLOUR COMBINATIONS

With the many new colours that have appeared over the years, there are many possible combinations for mating. Fortunately, the short gestation period of Syrian hamsters, combined with the fact that females can be used for breeding from four to five months of age, means that the results of a definite breeding plan can be seen very quickly, within a couple of years.

It is possible to embark on a breeding programme with a definite goal in mind. Some colours are readily available but others are much harder to obtain, so an exhibitor needs to consider whether he or she will embark on a long-term breeding programme to obtain the desired colour, or if he or she will try to keep a colour line robust so that it conforms to the Standard. Most colours have an alternative colour to which they can be mated in order to achieve another colour, although the desired colour will not appear until the second (F2) generation.

Some colours that have appeared are natural mutations, while others have been the result of deliberately combining two, three or four naturally mutated colours. It is possible to remake these combination colours from scratch, provided all the naturally mutated original colours can be obtained. Mating two naturally mutated colours will result in original-coloured offspring, but mating two of these should produce some hamsters of the desired colour.

NATURAL COLOUR MUTATIONS
- Black
- Black Eyed Cream
- Cinnamon
- Dark Eared White
- Dark Grey
- Golden
- Light Grey
- Rust
- Sepia
- Silver Grey
- Yellow

143

TWO-COLOUR COMBINATIONS
- Beige (Rust X Dark Grey)
- Black Eyed Ivory (Black Eyed Cream X Light Grey or Dark Grey)
- Black Eyed White (Black Eyed Cream X White Bellied Gene or Dominant Spot)
- Blonde (Light Grey X Cinnamon)
- Caramel (Rust X Black Eyed Cream)
- Chocolate (Black) (Rust X Black)
- Dove (Cinnamon X Black)
- Flesh Eared White (Cinnamon X Dark Eared White)
- Honey (Cinnamon X Yellow)
- Lilac (Cinnamon X Dark Grey)
- Melanistic Yellow (Yellow X Black)
- Red Eyed Cream (Black Eyed Cream X Cinnamon)
- Sable (Black Eyed Cream X Umbrous Gene)
- Smoke Pearl (Dark Grey X Yellow)
- Tortoiseshell (Yellow X Coloured animal)

THREE-COLOUR COMBINATIONS
- Chocolate (Sable) (Black Eyed Cream X Rust X Umbrous Gene)
- Lilac Pearl (Dark Grey X Yellow X Cinnamon)
- Mink (Black Eyed Cream X Cinnamon X Umbrous Gene)
- Red Eyed Ivory (Black Eyed Cream X Cinnamon X Light Grey or Dark Grey)
- Tortoiseshell and White (Yellow X Any Colour X Spot or Band)

FOUR-COLOUR COMBINATIONS
- Copper (Black Eyed Cream X Umbrous Gene X Rust X Cinnamon)
- Blue Mink (Black Eyed Cream X Cinnamon X Umbrous Gene X Dark Grey).

PRINCIPLES OF COLOUR BREEDING
The Umbrous gene can be combined with any colour, with the exception of any colour that already contains the Umbrous gene. The Umbrous gene gives the animal an overall sooty appearance, and is sometimes referred to as the 'sooty' gene.

Similarly, the White Bellied gene can be combined with any colour, although this will produce two distinct colours. An Agouti hamster carrying the gene will be White Bellied, whereas a self-coloured hamster with the same gene will be a Roan.

Light Grey and Rust are both natural mutations that are infrequently seen on the show bench. With both colours in low numbers, it is not surprising that Beige, Copper and Blonde are also seldom seen – Light Grey is needed in the genetic make-up of Blonde, while Rust is needed to produce Beige and Copper.

Natural mutations carrying a single colour gene are generally more 'robust', with the exception of Dark Grey. The more 'delicate' Dark Grey benefits from being mated back to the more robust Golden from time to time. Similarly, hamsters that have received one colour gene from Dark Grey (Smoke Pearl, Beige, Lilac) would also benefit from mating back to the more robust second colour in their genetic make-up. It is worthwhile 'sacrificing' the colour for one generation, to keep the line healthy and strong.

To specialise in one of the more unusual colours, such as Smoke Pearl or Lilac, you will need a number of different coloured hamsters, even if you already have some hamsters of the desired colour. The selection of different colours is vital to ensure that size, strength and colour remain of the highest quality. For example, if we are breeding for Smoke Pearl, we need a breeding base of Smoke Pearls, Dark Greys, Yellows and a Golden, unless we know we can 'borrow' a hamster of the right colour from another exhibitor. Similarly, Lilac would need Lilacs, Dark Greys, Cinnamons and a Golden. The Golden is required, in both cases, to keep the Dark Grey contribution robust. Having kept and exhibited these colours for many years, our experience has shown that these combinations help to keep the incidence of kinked tails as low as possible, as well as helping to strengthen the body frame.

Creams (both Black and Red Eyed), Cinnamons, and Yellows are robust colours, which rarely need injections of a different colour to keep the line strong. To prevent inbreeding, new hamsters of the same colour can be introduced from time to time. We recommend that anyone intending to breed hamsters for the first time should initially choose a robust colour until the ramifications of breeding some of the more unusual colours is understood. Black Eyed Cream to Sable Band, or Black Eyed Cream Band to Sable makes an excellent first mating for the novice, giving a variety of colours (Black Eyed Cream, Black Eyed Cream Band, Sable, and Sable Band) without compromising the genetic integrity of those colours. If one of the parents in this example is Satin, then the resultant offspring may also contain some Satin coats.

Genetics is a highly complex subject, and it has only been dealt with in the simplest of terms in this chapter. If you are seriously interested in breeding, and would like to know more about the genetic principles behind breeding for colours, we suggest that you read one of the many specialist books on the subject.

CHAPTER 11

BREEDING CHINESE AND DWARF HAMSTERS

1. Breeding Chinese
2. A note before breeding Dwarfs
3. Breeding Campbells
4. Breeding Winter Whites
5. Breeding Roborovskis
6. Fostering and hand-rearing
7. Record keeping
8. Colours and patterns
9. Simple genetics
10. Colour combinations

Many people who breed Dwarf and Chinese hamsters do so because they have chosen to keep a mixed-sex pair and nature has taken care of the rest. Although Dwarf and Chinese hamsters have slightly smaller litters than Syrians, once breeding has begun, litters will continue to arrive on a regular basis. Indeed, some pairs might produce young at a seemingly impossible rate!

The females normally give birth and raise their young with few problems, while the males also help to rear their young. The sight of mum, dad and babies interacting is fascinating and sometimes very amusing. It is one of the most rewarding aspects of keeping these hamsters.

The babies of Chinese and Dwarf hamsters are much smaller than their Syrian cousins, and are mobile at an earlier age. Therefore, you must give special consideration to the choice of cage. It may be necessary to take precautions to prevent escape by the wandering babies. Strips of cardboard (about 2 inches or 5 cms high) placed strategically around the cage where the base meets the wire top, will help prevent early exploration of the outside world.

You must also consider what will happen to the litters you intend to breed. A local pet shop may be willing to take some of the babies, but it is best to check this out before you allow males and females to live in the same cage. If you are a member of a hamster club you may be able to sell your babies at one of their shows. Never allow a mixed-sex pair to share a cage unless you know you can find homes for the many young they will produce.

1. BREEDING CHINESE

If you want to breed Chinese hamsters you will need a single breeding pair or a mixed colony. If you are breeding to improve your stock for exhibiting, you may find it worthwhile to keep pairs, rather than colonies, as the parents can be chosen by you. In a colony, the parentage of the offspring cannot be controlled or traced with any certainty, which is important if you are keeping accurate records.

Whether you are keeping pairs or colonies, the hamsters will need to be introduced at an early age, four to eight weeks being the ideal. Any later, and compatibility problems could occur. Most hamsters will not accept the sudden addition of a new hamster to their cage.

Chinese hamsters do not reproduce as regularly as Dwarf hamsters, with the gap between litters sometimes being quite long. However, it is also the case that, given the right conditions, these little hamsters can breed surprisingly quickly. Should you wish to breed throughout the year you will need to adjust the cage environment to simulate the conditions (e.g. temperature and daylight hours) found in the hamster's natural habitat (see chapter ten).

COLONIES

If you intend to keep a colony to breed from, you will need a large cage with plenty of room, so that each hamster has its own space to retire to should the need arise. The ideal ratio for a colony is two males to every three females. A trio of one male and two females is not recommended. The female hamster is always more dominant than the male, and a male kept with two females can become so 'henpecked' that his life is a misery. In addition, if one of the females develops a very strong bond with the male, the other female can become the butt of a great deal of aggression. A group comprised of two males to every three females will still have the occasional squabble, but it is unlikely that any one individual will be bullied to the point that it has to be removed from the group. It is worth noting, however, that any group containing more than one female will probably result in one of the females trying to gain supremacy over the others. This matriarch may try to prevent the other females from breeding, and, if they manage to produce a litter, she might take the babies to rear herself.

MIXED PAIRS

As mentioned earlier, the female is the more dominant of the two sexes, and this can lead to occasional problems in a mixed pair group. The female can become very aggressive towards the male, especially during the latter part of her pregnancy. The female's normal expression of aggression is to bite the male's rear end, sometimes causing serious injury. This behaviour has led to speculation about the natural social grouping of Chinese hamsters. It is possible, though not proven, that they do not live in colonies in their natural habitat, choosing instead to live separately but in close proximity to one another. Over the years, we have kept some pairs that lived in complete harmony, while others had to be split up due to the female's physical aggression towards the male.

PAIRINGS/COLONIES TO AVOID

Although we can find no definitive evidence that the Dominant Spot Chinese carries the Eyeless White gene, we believe that it is not worth taking the chance that it does not. If you intend to breed Dominant Spots, we recommend that only one of the breeding pair should be a Dominant Spot. Likewise, colonies should be composed so that only the males, or only the females, are Dominant Spots.

PREGNANCY
Females become sexually mature at around three months, although the male may have been seen to mount the female prior to this time. The normal gestation period is 20 to 21 days, although shorter periods have been recorded. Unfortunately, because of this variation in gestation, predicting the day of birth is very difficult, if not impossible. Often, the female is only noticeably pregnant in the last day of gestation, and in some cases the pregnancy may not be evident at all. Sometimes, the first indication of a litter is the sound of squeaking from the nest. If there is a chance that your female Chinese is pregnant, you should always take great care when cleaning the cage. It is not unknown for a litter to be deposited in the rubbish bin before being discovered and then hastily returned to the cage!

BIRTH
Most females will give birth with few, if any, problems. Although it is difficult, you should resist the temptation to keep checking the nest to see if the mother has given birth without difficulty, as the female will be greatly distressed by this. Chinese hamsters are naturally shy and timid, and disturbances during pregnancy, or in the first days following birth, may result in the mother destroying her litter.

When the female gives birth, she will normally produce four to six babies, all born blind and naked. As with Syrian hamsters, there may be some blood on the bedding, but this is perfectly normal and nothing to worry about.

The female may expel the male from the nest shortly before the birth, during birth, or shortly afterwards. However, she will normally allow him back in the nest once the babies have started to grow, so that he can help with their care.

THE BABIES
Although the babies are born blind and naked, their markings become visible as early as three days of age, and by seven days the fur is apparent. At one week old, the babies may be seen emerging from the nest, although their protective parents will probably retrieve them very quickly. At approximately 14 days, the babies' eyes will open, and, by 18 to 21 days, the babies are independent and could be transferred to a cage of their own.

FEEDING
A mixture of wheat germ, first-stage dried baby food, small broken particles of hamster food, and some small birdseed is ideal as baby food. This can be sprinkled on the babies from the seventh day onwards.

HANDLING
Handling can start at 14 days, but be prepared for the speed and agility of the babies. You may find it extremely difficult to catch the babies in order to handle them. It is, therefore, advisable to use a large, high-sided cardboard box when handling the babies, remembering not to lift them too far from the bottom in case

they jump. It is also worth mentioning that Chinese hamsters are liable to run up your arms as often as they run off your hand, so be prepared for this as well.

Some parents can be fiercely protective of their young. If you try to begin handling at 14 days and the parents object, you may need to defer handling for a couple more days.

SEPARATING PARENTS AND BABIES
Chinese babies are independent a little earlier than their Syrian counterparts, usually between 18 and 21 days. Some breeders remove the babies at this age, to avoid any problems from the mother should she have another litter due imminently. If the babies are separated from their parents at 18 to 21 days, the sexes do not need to be segregated straight away. Chinese hamsters reach sexual maturity a little later than their Syrian counterparts, and can be safely housed together for the first 7 or 8 weeks of life. Most Chinese hamsters do not reach sexual maturity until three to four months of age, but it is best not to get too close to this time limit unless you intend to keep the babies together in a breeding colony.

If the female is not pregnant again, and you want to leave the babies with their parents for a little longer, you will find that that the two generations will live in harmony for some time, provided that the cage is large enough. However, as soon as the female babies reach sexual maturity, it is likely that their brothers and their father will try to mate with them, which may cause problems if you do not want another litter, or if you are trying to follow a specific breeding programme. If you want to separate the babies from their parents, but would prefer to allow them more time in their parents' care, you should separate them safely from about four weeks of age.

2. A NOTE BEFORE BREEDING DWARFS
The Campbell, Winter White and Roborovski hamsters have very similar breeding habits and requirements. However, it is worth mentioning that the different species should not be kept together for breeding. The resulting hybrid offspring may carry genetic defects, and, if they keep producing young, they could alter the genetic purity of the different species. It is a common myth that hybrid offspring, resulting from a mating between two hamsters of different species, are infertile. However, it only takes one or two exceptions to upset the genetic balance of a species.

Like Chinese hamsters, a pair or a colony of hamsters should be introduced at an early age, one to two months of age being ideal. Older males may accept a young female but take care during the settling-in period. It is very unlikely that an older female will accept a male of any age. Many breeders choose to keep pairs of Dwarf hamsters, as opposed to colonies. This is because fewer problems arise in a mixed-sex pair, and greater control can be exercised over breeding lines and quality.

As with all animals, breeding closely related parents could lead to genetic problems if done haphazardly, although experienced breeders will sometimes use related hamsters to emphasise a particular good feature of that line. If you are new to breeding, or inexperienced in genetics, do not attempt inbreeding.

Syrian and Chinese hamsters can be fooled into breeding at any time of the year, and the same applies to all the Dwarf species. You will need to adjust the temperature and the amount of daylight hours the hamster receives.

3. BREEDING CAMPBELLS

PAIRINGS TO AVOID

As with all varieties of hamster, certain combinations of parents should be avoided. One such pairing is that of Mottled and Mottled. This combination can produce an 'eyeless white' variety, so always mate a Mottled to a Non-Mottled. Mating satin Campbell to satin Campbell does not have any of the problems associated with the same type of mating in the Syrians, so this pairing can be allowed without problems.

DIABETES

Certain lines of Campbells are susceptible to diabetes. When we first began keeping hamsters there was no evidence of this condition in the UK. It is believed that the condition was introduced to the UK in the late 1980s, when the Albino Campbells was brought to the country, bred to other Campbells, and subsequently infected the resident UK stock. The onset of the disease has been linked to stress, and, as a consequence, some breeders move their Campbells around their hamstery, so that the hamsters do not become accustomed to one particular spot. Strange as this may seem, it appears to work. An animal that is used to change does not become as stressed as one that stays in one place and is unaccustomed to a sudden change.

A Campbell who develops diabetes will drink a great deal of water, and have an extensive wet corner. They may even develop a 'waist' or a pinched look around their middle, instead of the usual sleek, plump appearance of the Campbell. As with humans who suffer from diabetes, hamsters may also develop other complications associated with the disease, such as eye problems.

Where possible, prospective breeding pairs should be urine-tested for diabetes before being paired up and allowed to breed. This can be done using a testing-stick for diabetes, which can be obtained from a vet or a pharmacist. This is not an infallible test, but, if you start with a clear stock, there is every chance that they will remain clear, and, theoretically, their offspring should stand a better chance of being clear of the disease.

MATING

Over the last few years, some breeders have applied breeding techniques used with Syrian hamsters. Rather than keeping a mixed-sex pair or a colony, the hamsters are housed separately and introduced only when the breeder wants them to produce a litter. This has several benefits, including the ability to predict the birth more accurately, to restrict the number of litters the female has, and to allow for the use of a different male for each litter. We have used this method when our Campbells reproduced so quickly that they threatened to take over the whole house.

If you are worried about the strain on the female looking after a litter on her own, remember that this will be offset by the fact that she will not be pregnant while nursing her babies, and the longer gaps between litters, imposed by separation, can only be beneficial to her health and stamina.

If you want to try this approach, you will need to carefully supervise introductions between the desired mating pair. The two hamsters should be introduced nightly, on neutral ground, taking the same precautions used with Syrians (see page 113).

If you prefer the traditional approach of keeping Campbells in pairs or colonies, remember that a surprising number of offspring will be produced in a very short time. Normally, most females will not produce a litter until they are about three months old, but, if a young female is introduced to an older male, a litter could be expected sooner. On one occasion, we had a litter arrive when the female (paired to an older male) was only 43 days old, which, if you assume an 18-day gestation period, meant that she conceived at 25 days of age.

You should also consider the health of the female, as the strain of constant pregnancies and litter rearing can take its toll. Litter sizes seem to decrease when the female keeps producing continually, although it is quite common for three litters to arrive in quick succession, followed by a short break before another litter arrives. Females seem to stop conceiving at about 11 months of age, although there are always exceptions to the rules.

PREGNANCY

The gestation period for Campbells is between 18 and 20 days. However, many breeders have recorded delayed implantation, where the female of a pair has given birth to a litter up to four weeks after mating. Calculating the delivery date, therefore, will largely be a matter of guesswork, so cleaning the cage and handling should always be done carefully if you suspect a litter might be imminent.

BIRTH

Like the other hamster varieties, birth is normally straightforward. A little blood can be expected on the bedding, but this is normal. It is usual for the male to mate with his partner soon after the birth of the litter, so, if you want the female to produce one litter only, the male should be removed from the cage before the birth of the litter. However, bear in mind that once removed, the likelihood of reintroducing him successfully is remote.

If you intend to allow the male to stay, remember that, while the male may be allowed in the nest during the birth, he is normally banished soon after. However, the female should allow him to return to the nest within two to three days after the birth.

The average litter size for a Campbell is six, although larger litters are not uncommon and litters of 10 or more are not unknown. As a general rule, the older the female and the more she has reproduced, the smaller the litter size. Female Campbells normally make very good mothers, and, when the male is allowed back into the nest, he will help with the babies' care, by bringing food to the nest, helping to keep the babies warm, and retrieving any wandering offspring.

THE BABIES

The babies are born blind and naked. At three or four days old the babies' fur can be seen and at eight days the babies look like miniatures of their parents, apart from the fact that their eyes remain closed. At approximately 14 days, the babies' eyes will open and the babies will become increasingly mobile. By 18 days of age, the babies are normally independent of their parents.

CAGE CLEANING

Once the babies are approximately 12 days old, you can clean the cage. Put the mother and father out to play before you begin. Do not clean the cage too thoroughly as this is likely to upset the parents. Simply remove the soiled shavings and any uneaten food, and leave the nest area alone. Add fresh food and water, and sprinkle some birdseed around the food dish. This will help to distract the parents once they are returned to the cage.

Once you have returned the parents, leave the group undisturbed for an hour or two, while the parents settle down, check their babies, and investigate the cleaned cage. Some mothers resent having the cage cleaned and try to rearrange the nest. You may spot the mother carrying a baby around the cage, not knowing where to put it. However, given a little time and some privacy, the mother will always settle down after this frantic activity.

Once the babies reach 16 days old and are a little more independent, you can clean the cage thoroughly. This will allow you to make preparations for the next litter, which can be expected very shortly if you are keeping both parents together.

HANDLING
The babies can be handled from 14 days, once their eyes are open. The parents may take exception to your handling the babies, trying to 'box' your hand with their front paws. This is normal and nothing to worry about, but if the 'boxing' turns into an attempt to bite, it is best to leave handling for another day or two.

When you first handle the babies, they may protest by producing tiny chattering sounds. The babies are likely to be very nervous and jumpy, so extreme caution should be taken.

Always handle the babies a little above the floor level, so that they cannot fall too far if they jump or fall. It is also advisable to handle in a secure area, such as a cardboard box, so that any escapees will be restricted to the confines of the box.

SEPARATING PARENTS AND BABIES
Campbell hamsters are independent of their parents from approximately 18 days. It is very common for the mother to produce another litter 18 days after giving birth previously, and many youngsters find themselves expelled from the nest at this point. In the event of the mother becoming aggressive towards the older litter, you may need to remove the older litter to a cage of their own. However, this is not always necessary, and if the parents allow them to stay, the older babies will help to care for their younger siblings, becoming very protective of them. On one occasion, while trying to look into a nest of newborn babies, our fingers were totally ignored by the parents but thoroughly 'boxed' by several of the previous litter we had left in the cage.

If the older litter is allowed to remain in the cage with their parents and the new litter, it is advisable to allow this for approximately 10 days only. You should remove the older litter at approximately 28 days, to avoid any unwanted pregnancies caused by the father mating with his daughters. The litter can normally be kept together until they are six or seven weeks old, at which point they may start to reproduce among themselves. If you have the cage space, it is wise to separate the sexes at this age, in case new homes are not found for them for some time.

4. BREEDING WINTER WHITES
Winter Whites follow the same pattern as their Campbell cousins, in nearly all aspects of breeding and raising their young.

152

THE BREEDING PAIR

Many breeders find that a pair of Winter Whites is preferable to a colony, as the females tend to attack the males if there are too many of them. Winter Whites will normally stop breeding at around 11 months of age, but we recently heard of a female that produced her first litter after her first birthday. A breeder had kept the female as a pet and when she reached 12 months old (presumably past breeding age), she was found a partner to live with in her old age. Not only did the pair settle down with none of the usual squabbles associated with such a late introduction, but, within four weeks, an unexpected litter was produced. To astound her owner even further, she produced a second litter at 15 months of age.

PAIRINGS TO AVOID

There are no colour restrictions in pairing Winter Whites. In the past, Pearl males were regarded as sterile in the UK, although fertile Pearls up to the age of about 12 weeks had been recorded. However, over the last few years, we have heard of many more older, fertile Pearl males.

One of our own Pearl males, Bamber, has just fathered his 11th litter at the age of 16 months, and, in total, he has fathered 68 offspring. In addition, his Pearl brother, some of his Pearl sons, and some of his Pearl grandsons, have been proved fertile after 12 weeks of age. It is possible that some Pearl males are infertile while others are not.

To produce a litter containing Pearls you may need to mate a Pearl female to a Normal Winter White male, but to get a Sapphire Pearl would involve selective mating over two generations, and is best left to more experienced breeders.

MATING

If you keep a colony or a mixed-sex pair, nature will take care of the rest. However, a more radical method has been tried of late, which is to introduce a mature pair and leave them together for several days (at least four). Although there has been some success with this method, extreme care must be taken during the initial introduction as fighting can occur. Only very experienced breeders should try this method, as they will know the temperament of their lines.

PREGNANCY AND BIRTH

As the gestation period for the Winter White is between 18 and 20 days, and delayed implantation has also been recorded, the actual date of birth will be uncertain. Cage cleaning and handling should always be done very carefully if you suspect a litter is due. Like Campbell females, Winter White females normally give birth without difficulty, and it is usual for the male to mate with his female partner soon after. Should you wish to experience the joy of one litter only, the male should be removed from the cage before the birth. However, reintroducing the male might be almost impossible.

THE BABIES

Winter White females make good mothers, and, if the father is allowed to remain in the nest, he will help to rear his offspring.

The babies follow a similar developmental pattern to their Campbell cousins, and are normally independent at approximately 18 days. As with Campbells, the cage can be semi-cleaned 12 days after the birth, and handling can begin at 14 days, once the babies' eyes are open, if the parents are amenable.

5. BREEDING ROBOROVSKIS

Although Roborovskis have been kept as pets since the early 1990s, information regarding their breeding habits is still very scarce. It appears that the longer they have been kept in captivity, the more their breeding habits are changing, but there is still some inconsistency in breeding patterns.

The first Roborovskis kept in captivity did not breed before the age of nine months, and, even today, breeding may not begin until the female is about 10 months old. Once breeding has started, three or four litters may follow in quick succession, with the last litter arriving when the female is approximately 14 months.

However, over recent years, more breeding pairs are following the pattern exhibited by the other Dwarf varieties, by beginning to breed at three to four months of age. One of the earliest-born litters was recorded when the female was just 10 weeks old, which meant the female conceived around seven weeks of age.

MIXED PAIRS

Due to their small size, it is preferable to house a breeding pair of Roborovskis in a tank (glass or plastic) rather than a barred cage. The babies are so tiny that even the narrowest-barred cages may not be secure enough to contain any wandering infants.

PAIRINGS TO AVOID

As present, no colour or coat mutations are known. Therefore, pairing these hamsters presents little problem. However, as with all varieties of hamsters, inbreeding should be avoided.

PREGNANCY AND BIRTH

Gestation lasts between 20 and 23 days. Litters are normally slightly smaller than the other Dwarfs, numbering between three and five babies on average. Very few litters are born with more than this. A period of four weeks between litters is not uncommon.

THE BABIES

The babies are born naked and blind, with fur beginning to show at around four days. The babies start to resemble their parents and become mobile at seven to eight days. At 14 days, their eyes will open and they look like miniatures of their parents. At 21 days, they are independent, but, if left with their parents, they normally live in harmony with the next litter.

Baby Roborovskis can be extremely difficult to sex, largely due to their size. Many experienced breeders have this problem and usually wait until the babies are a little older before confirming the sex of each one.

HANDLING

Handling baby Robos requires even greater care than handling other baby hamsters. Baby Robos are incredibly quick, which makes them difficult to control. A handling container of some sort is a definite must.

6. FOSTERING AND HAND-REARING

Although it is rare for Dwarf or Chinese hamsters to be fostered or hand-reared, it is not unknown. Follow the guidelines laid out in the previous chapter on Syrians, making allowances for the smaller size of Chinese and Dwarf babies.

The chances of fostering or hand-rearing Dwarf and Chinese babies successfully are not great, but it is always worth trying. It takes only one success to make it worthwhile.

7. RECORD KEEPING

It is vital that you keep records of the hamsters you breed. This will allow you to choose the right pairings for certain colours, and it will also ensure that you are choosing healthy animals of the right age for breeding. Your records should follow the format described on page 129.

If you keep your hamsters in a colony, you will find it very difficult to keep accurate records of births and parentage. If more than one male is kept in the colony, the identity of the father will be questionable. The identity of the mother may also be uncertain unless each of the females in the colony has a distinguishing feature that enables you to identify her. Another problem that can thwart accurate record keeping is that two females in a colony that give birth around the same time may decide to create a communal crèche.

If you keep a mixed-sex pair, it is much easier to keep accurate records. The arrival of babies may pass unnoticed for a day or two, making it difficult to establish the precise date of birth, but the date you notice them will be precise enough not to matter.

8. COLOURS AND PATTERNS

In this section, the colours and patterns are described in general terms, to give the reader an idea of what the hamster looks like. If you are going to exhibit your hamster and join one of the many hamster clubs around the world, you

will be given a list of Standards, to which your hamster should conform. Each colour has a different Standard, and unfortunately, the Standards differ slightly between different clubs and different countries. Furthermore, some of the colours described here have not, at time of writing, been accepted as a Standard colour, although they are fairly common. Conversely, some of the accepted Standard colours may now be quite rare. The descriptions given here are very general; they are not intended to replace the Standards laid out by each individual club. If you intend to show your hamster, you will need to join a club and ask for the club's official Standards.

TERMINOLOGY
To help you to follow the colour descriptions, there first follows a brief explanation of the terminology used:
- **Ticking:** The endmost tip of each individual hair is a contrasting colour to the rest. Ticking is not present in all hamsters.
- **Topcoat:** The fur between the tip of the hair and the base colour of the hair, i.e. the middle of the hair. In a hamster that has no ticking, the tip and the topcoat are the same colour.

- **Base colour:** The bottom part of each individual hair (i.e. the part nearest the skin) is a different colour from the rest. Not all hamsters have a base colour – some hamsters' fur is the same colour from root to tip, but if a base colour is present, it can be seen by blowing gently on the topcoat to part it.
- **Belly fur:** The coat fur covering the underside of the hamster, between its four legs.
- **Arches:** These are found on each side of the hamster. They separate the topcoat from the belly fur and resemble arches, hence their name. Arches are not present on all hamsters.
- **Dorsal Stripe:** This is also known as the Spinal Stripe. It is a stripe of a different colour to the rest of the fur. It runs the length of the hamster's back, from between the eyes to the base of the tail.

CAMPBELL COLOURS AND PATTERNS

NORMAL
This hamster has a brown-grey topcoat with dark-brown ticking, giving an overall appearance of buff-coloured brown fur with cream carried about a third of the way down the hair. The base colour is very dark slate grey, and the off-white belly fur has a slate-grey base colour. This hamster has three arches of pale amber, a black dorsal stripe, grey-brown ears, black eyes, and off-white feet. This is the colour most commonly seen in pet shops.

ALBINO
This hamster's fur is totally white, having no arches or dorsal stripe. Its eyes are bright pink and its ears are flesh coloured. This colour is frequently seen for sale in pet shops or on the sales table at hamster shows.

ARGENTÉ
A light-cinnamon topcoat with a smoky-grey base colour gives this hamster a very pretty appearance. The belly fur is creamy white with a smoky-grey base coat, and there should be three clearly defined arches. The spinal stripe is smoky grey, the eyes red, and the ears flesh coloured. The feet are creamy, with a white base colour. This colour is now more readily available.

BLACK
This hamster has a black topcoat, sometimes with a silvering effect in the coat that becomes more obvious with age. There are no arches but the dorsal stripe, although black, can be noticeable against the topcoat. The eyes are black and the ears dark grey. The belly fur is black with a white flash on the throat. Although this colour is relatively new, it is becoming easier to find at hamster shows, although it may not be that common in pet shops.

DOVE
A Dove-coloured hamster has a pinky-grey to sandy-grey topcoat. As Black forms part of its genetic make-up, a silvering effect may also be seen. The dorsal stripe is brown and the arches are absent. The eyes are red and the ears light grey. This colour is still comparatively rare, even at hamster shows.

OPAL
The topcoat is a blue-grey colour, with ivory arches and a charcoal-grey dorsal stripe. The eyes are black and the ears pinkish grey. This colour is fairly difficult to acquire, at present.

HARLEQUIN
The Harlequin hamster has patches of two different colours. Popular combinations are Normal/Argenté and Dove/Black. Unfortunately, this particular patterning is still fairly rare.

PLATINUM
The topcoat is a brown-grey colour. White ticking is found throughout the coat but may be heavier across the shoulders. The amount of ticking varies between hamsters, from very little to an almost-white animal. The base colour is very dark slate grey. Where the white ticking is not so pronounced, the dorsal stripe is black and the arches appear amber. The ears are dark grey and the eyes are black. Platinum hamsters are gaining popularity very quickly, with numbers increasing all the time.

PLATINUM ARGENTÉ
This colour is the same as the Argenté, but with influences from the Platinum colour, such as white ticking throughout the coat, which is sometimes heavier across the shoulders. The dorsal stripe, arches, eyes and ears are all the same as the Argenté. Again, this is a colour that is gaining in popularity.

PLATINUM BLACK
The Platinum Black is similar to the standard Black, but the silvering effect or white ticking is accentuated by the platinum gene. This colour can vary greatly, from a nearly black hamster to an almost-platinum one. Like the Platinum, the Platinum Black is highly sought after, its striking good looks appealing to many hamster keepers.

WHITE (BLACK EYED)
As the name suggests, this hamster is white, with no arches or a dorsal stripe. However, the coat may contain some dark hairs. The eyes are black and the ears are flesh coloured, with dark grey spotting or patches. This colour is not seen for sale very often.

WHITE BELLIED
The overall appearance is that of a Normal-coloured hamster but with white belly fur. As these hamsters carry the White Bellied gene, care must be taken when breeding. Mating two White Bellied hamsters together can produce Eyeless White hamsters, as happens with Syrians.

MOTTLED
This is a coloured hamster with irregular patches of white. The eye colour ranges from bright red to very dark red, depending on the hamster's basic coat colour. It is almost certain that these hamsters carry the White Bellied gene, so precautions should be taken when breeding from them.

CAMPBELL COAT TYPES

SATIN
This coat type has a totally different appearance to the Syrian version. The overall look is that of an ordinary Dwarf hamster with damp fur. It is available in many colours.

REX
The coat of a Rex is soft, close, and frizzy in appearance. The whiskers are curly. At present, the fur is very sparse and gives the hamster an almost bald appearance.

WINTER WHITE COLOURS AND PATTERNS

NORMAL
The topcoat is grey to brown with black ticking, giving an overall appearance of greyish brown. It has a base colour of extremely dark slate blue, and clear white belly fur with a blue-tinged base colour. There are three clearly defined arches separating the top colour and the belly fur. This hamster also has a black dorsal stripe, grey ears with a pinkish tone, black eyes, and off-white feet. This hamster is more commonly seen at hamster shows than in pet shops.

PEARL (NORMAL)
This is a white hamster, lightly and evenly ticked with black guard hairs. The belly fur is white, the ears are grey and the eyes are black.

PEARL (SAPPHIRE)
The only difference between the Sapphire Pearl and the Normal Pearl is that the former has much lighter ticking and lighter-coloured ears.

SAPPHIRE
The topcoat on this hamster is a soft, smoky grey with a blue tinge. The base coat is steel blue. The belly fur is off-white with a bluish tinge, separated from the topcoat by three arches. It has a steel-blue dorsal stripe, black eyes, pastel-grey ears and off-white feet. This colour is more often seen at hamster shows than in pet shops.

CHINESE COLOURS AND PATTERNS

NORMAL
The Normal-coloured Chinese hamster has a brownish-grey topcoat with dark-brown ticking and a slate-grey under colour. The belly fur is off-white with a slate-grey under colour. It has black eyes and dark-brown ears with off-white rims. There is a black dorsal stripe and a well-defined line along the sides.

DOMINANT SPOT
This is basically a Normal-coloured hamster with white spots. The spotting can range from one or two small spots to an almost-white animal. In some extreme cases, the spotting has been so complete as to lead breeders to believe that a new colour (Black Eyed White) has appeared, but, if these hamsters are bred to a Normal, Dominant Spots appear in the resulting litter.

ROBOROVSKI COLOURS AND PATTERNS

NORMAL
This is the only colour available at the moment. The topcoat is a sandy gold with a slate-grey under coat. The belly fur and arches are pure white, but there is no dorsal stripe. The Robo also has pure white 'eyebrows' above its black eyes, and its muzzle is also pure white. The combination of the white facial markings gives these markings a very appealing expression.

9. SIMPLE GENETICS
The same genetic terms described in the chapter on breeding Syrians apply to both Dwarf and Chinese hamsters (see pages 130-131). On the whole, the genetics behind Dwarf and Chinese breeding principles follow the same rules as the Syrian, with one exception – the Satin gene of the Campbell is recessive.

10. COLOUR COMBINATIONS

CHINESE
Although the Chinese have been in the Western world far longer than any of the Dwarf hamsters, only one natural colour mutation, the Dominant Spot, has occurred. Being a dominant gene, one of the parents has to visibly exhibit this gene for offspring to inherit the spotting.

CAMPBELL
In recent years, the Campbell has produced many new colour mutations and two coat mutations (Satin and Rex). At present, the Rex coat is very fine and sparse, sometimes giving the appearance of an almost bald hamster. Unlike the Syrian, the Satin gene is recessive in the Campbell, meaning that two Satin Campbells can be mated together without any of the possible coat problems that could occur if two Satin Syrian hamsters were mated. Mating Satin to Satin should give 100 per cent Satin in the resultant litter. Pattern genes (Mottled and Platinum) are both dominant genes.

NATURAL COLOUR MUTATIONS
• Albino
• Argenté
• Black
• Mottled
• Normal
• Opal
• Platinum

COLOUR AND PATTERN COMBINATIONS
• Argenté Mottled (Argenté X Mottled)
• Argenté Platinum (Argenté X Platinum)
• Black Eyed White (Normal X Platinum X Diluting gene)
• Black Mottled (Black X Mottled)

- Black Platinum (Black X Platinum)
- Dove (Argenté X Black)
- Dove Mottled (Argenté X Black X Mottled)
- Harlequin (Normal X Argenté)
- Normal Mottled (Normal X Mottled)
- Opal Mottled (Opal X Mottled)

WINTER WHITE

The Winter White has not produced as many colours as the Campbell, either by natural mutation or by combining naturally mutated colours. There are no coat mutations in the Winter White hamsters to date.

NATURAL COLOUR MUTATIONS
- Normal
- Pearl (Normal Pearl)
- Sapphire

COLOUR COMBINATIONS

To date, the Sapphire Pearl is the only colour combination that we know of. It is not straightforward to breed, due to the fact that two generations are needed to produce a Sapphire Pearl. In the following example, we have used a Normal Pearl female, because fertile Pearl males may not be readily available.

- **First generation:** mating a Pearl female to a Sapphire male should produce 50 per cent Normal and 50 per cent Normal Pearl, all carrying the Sapphire gene.
- **Second generation:** mating a Normal Pearl female (carrying Sapphire) to a Sapphire male should produce 25 per cent Normal (carrying Sapphire), 25 per cent Normal Pearl (carrying Sapphire), 25 per cent Sapphire, and 25 per cent Sapphire Pearl.

ROBOROVSKI

There are no colour, coat or pattern mutations of this species at the present time.

CHAPTER 12

SHOWING YOUR HAMSTER

1. Joining a club
2. Showing for beginners
3. Show structure
4. The pet section
5. The Syrian section
6. The Dwarf (or Other Species) section

Human nature being what it is, everyone who owns a hamster naturally considers theirs to be the best in the world. This applies whether you have a single hamster or many. Therefore, a hamster show may be the only place a hamster's many good points will be appreciated objectively.

Hamster shows are gatherings where different hamsters are judged against each other. However, the shows offer far more than this. Part of the attraction is that everyone there shares the same enthusiasm for hamsters. It is also a place where you can see and buy some of the more rare colours, you can find out how to solve many hamster problems, and you will learn more about your beloved hamster.

1. JOINING A CLUB

You do not need to be a member of any club to show your hamster, although it can be very beneficial. By joining a club you will be advised about any forthcoming shows. Most clubs also supply their members with lists of Standards and details of how the hamsters will be judged. You will almost certainly get a regular journal or newsletter, providing you with the latest hamster news and tips on the many aspects of hamster keeping, exhibiting and breeding.

If you are interested in joining a hamster club, most now have their own websites, with details of how to contact them. However, if you do not have access to the Internet, you may be able to find contact addresses through libraries, pet shops, veterinary practices, or the appendix on page 170. We began showing in 1985, and it took us nearly six months to get details of a hamster club, and a further three months before we were able to exhibit for the first time. Today, most clubs post details of shows on their websites, together with a contact address or telephone number to obtain further details. Shows may also be advertised locally, in pet shops, libraries and halls.

Each hamster club has a show manager, who is responsible for arranging shows for the year. Details of these pre-arranged shows are normally presented at the club's annual general meeting (AGM). Traditionally, February, and sometimes January, have been left free of shows because of bad winter weather, but with the advent of better roads and road clearance, shows are now held in these months as well, so there is nearly always a show being held somewhere.

2. SHOWING FOR BEGINNERS

Most shows have a class for pet hamsters. Hamsters are judged on tameness and condition. The advantage of showing your hamster in this class, especially if you are new to exhibiting, is that you need only be at the show for a short period. Your first show will be a long day. By entering the pet class you can learn about hamster shows without overwhelming yourself. You will quickly learn that exhibiting and judging hamsters is time-consuming, demanding, and undertaken in a highly professional manner, even if there is a light-hearted atmosphere outside the judging area.

Your first time at a hamster show may be bewildering, but there are always plenty of officials and club members willing to help and to put you at your ease. Never be afraid to ask questions about what is going on – hamster fanciers love talking about hamsters with fellow enthusiasts.

If you are interested in taking up showing, but you are reluctant to exhibit at your very first show, attend a few shows as a spectator. Most clubs welcome the general public to their shows, inviting them to browse around and ask questions.

3. SHOW STRUCTURE

Most hamster shows are run along the same basic lines whichever club is holding the event. Each show normally has three separate sections:
• Pet section.
• Syrian section.
• Dwarf (or Other Species) section.

Each section has a judge, a book steward (who records the judge's marks), and a pen steward (who is responsible for the pens containing the hamsters). The show secretary for the day deals with all the paperwork and keeps track of the results.

4. THE PET SECTION

The Pet section is usually open to anyone – child or adult – who has a pet hamster. The owner does not have to be a member of the club and will not need to enter in advance. Entry is on the day, and, as long as the hamster arrives before the judging finishes, it will be judged. Posters usually give the time of judging, but, if in doubt, there is always a contact number on the poster to telephone to establish this.

When you arrive at the show, seek out the show secretary. The show secretary's table is usually quite obvious by the mounds of paperwork piled high on it, but you will be directed to the table if you cannot find it. You will need to give the secretary your details, and there is normally a small fee payable. Once you have paid your fee, you will be given a pen label to put on your hamster's cage and you will be told where you should place your pet. The pen label will carry an identification number, which will be used by the judge as a reference when judging. Once you have entered and placed your hamster in the correct place, you will be free to enjoy the rest of the show.

JUDGING
Pet hamsters are normally judged on condition and tameness. The judge will usually consider many things under the term 'condition'. When we judge the Pet section at hamster shows, we normally look for a good level of general health. For example, is the hamster too thin? Are the teeth overgrown? Are the toenails overlong? Are the eyes clear and bright? Condition is not necessarily the same as appearance, however. A hamster with one eye, or a hamster with three legs, stands as good a chance of winning as an able-bodied hamster, provided that it is in good health and has obviously been well cared for.

Once judging has finished, the Pet section judge is usually available to answer questions about your hamster. You may also find a note on your hamster's cage, asking you to "please see judge". This is normally nothing to be concerned about. It could mean anything; the judge may want to know your hamster's age, to advise you that your hamster's teeth are a bit long, or simply to ask you where you bought your hamster. It is surprising how many pet owners discover that Henry is really a Henrietta, or vice versa, at the end of the show – but this makes no difference to your hamster, as it already knows!

Club members are dedicated to the welfare of hamsters, so there are normally many leaflets available to help with feeding and general care. Many clubs give a certificate to everyone that enters, so that everyone goes away with an award of some kind. The winner may also receive a rosette or small trophy. Once the presentations are made, the owners are free to collect their hamsters and leave the show.

5. THE SYRIAN SECTION
Any hamster shown in this section must normally be entered in advance, although some clubs may accept late entries. Full details of the show, including the name of the show secretary, the available classes, the closing date for entries, and directions to the venue, will be found on the show schedule. Schedules are available from club secretaries, and may be posted on the Internet. If you belong to a club, you will receive schedules on a regular basis, a few weeks prior to the show date.

CLASSES
The main categories in the Syrian section are:
• Straight class
• Duplicate class
• Non-Standard class.
Each of these classes will have several subclasses, which will vary between clubs. If

you are in any doubt about which class your hamster should be entered into, the show secretary will normally be able to guide you.

STRAIGHT CLASS

Straight classes are designed to judge similar hamsters against one another. For example, Golden hamsters will be measured against other Golden hamsters, to choose the best example of that colour.

Every hamster that conforms to an accepted Standard colour must be entered into the Straight class. Straight classes are divided into shorthaired, longhaired, and satin-coated subclasses. The shorthaired and longhaired classes cover all the accepted Standard colours. Satin-coated hamsters usually have different classes, regardless of whether the animal is patterned or not. Some classes include one colour alone, while others will include several, such as the Any Other Colours (AOC) class, which covers colours and patterns not already covered by a Standard class.

DUPLICATE CLASS

Before any animal is entered into any of the Duplicate classes it must be entered into the appropriate Straight class. While the Straight classes judge hamsters of the same type against each other (e.g. shorthaired Cinnamons are measured against other shorthaired Cinnamons), the Duplicate Class allows hamsters from different Straight classes to be measured against each other, although the hamsters are not judged for a second time (see below). The purpose of this is to find the best hamster in each Duplicate class, regardless of colour, pattern or coat type.

Duplicate classes vary from club to club, but most have classes for juniors, novices and breeders. The Junior class is for exhibitors under the age of 16, the Novice class is for members in their first year of exhibiting, while the Breeder class is for hamsters bred by the exhibitor. There may be other Duplicate classes, but, as these vary from club to club, you will need to find out further details from the show secretary.

NON-STANDARD CLASS

Any hamster that does not conform to a Standard colour should be entered into the Non-Standard class. It cannot be entered into any of the Straight or Duplicate classes. Hamsters entered into the Non-Standard class may include a new colour that has yet to be made Standard, an Umbrous version of any of the existing colours, or a White Bellied animal. Our first hamster, Gorgeous, was one such Non-Standard. Judges desperately tried to fit her into a Standard colour, thumbing through their Standards Book to see if they could match her to a not-often-seen colour.

As all the animals in this class have no colour Standard, they cannot go on to enter the Duplicate class and win Best In Show. However, hamsters in the Non-Standard class are judged in the same way as hamsters in the Straight class, the exception being that they are not awarded a mark for colour and markings. The Non-Standard class is usually the last class to be judged. This is in case the judge finds a hamster in the Straight class that he or she deems to be a Non-Standard colour. The hamster can be reclassified to the Non-Standard class, so that it still has the opportunity to be judged.

FIRST-TIME ENTRANTS

As mentioned earlier, if you want to enter your hamster in a Straight class, you will probably need to enter in advance of the show date. Ask the show secretary which class your hamster should be entered into. You can do this by post or by telephone, but make sure you give as much information about your hamster as possible, including the colour, coat type and sex of each animal you want to enter. When you arrive at the show, there will also be plenty of officials willing to check that your hamster is in the right Straight class prior to placing it on the show bench.

To the uninitiated, a hamster show may look chaotic, but there is a definite order. Each section of the show has its own designated judging square. The pen stewards will place the exhibits in numerical order inside the judging square. Normally, the pen stewards are the only people allowed in the judging square, apart from the judge and the book steward (who notes the judge's marks). Each judge has his or her own preference as to which class they would like to judge first. The pen stewards will establish the judging order before judging commences, so that you know when your particular section will be judged. If you become confused at any point, one of the show officials will be more than happy to help you.

Once your hamster has been benched, you will not be allowed to return to it until the judging is complete. The main reason for this is to maintain the anonymity of the hamsters and exhibitors, based on the principle that anonymity equals fairness. The judge cannot show any favouritism if he or she does not know to whom each hamster belongs.

For the same reasons of fairness, all the hamsters are shown in identical pens, one hamster per pen. Each pen will display a label (the pen label) showing the hamster's entry number and a list of the Duplicate classes into which it has been entered. The show secretary is the only person (other than the owner) who knows the owner of the hamster in any given pen.

PRESENTATION

Showing pens are relatively expensive to purchase, so many clubs have pens that can be hired for the day. Other clubs allow animals to be shown in small plastic tanks, the design of which will be stipulated by the clubs concerned. In the UK, we prefer show pens, as the open wire fronts allow for the passage of air, even on warm days. Like plastic tanks, the clubs will lay down the specification of the show pens.

Shorthaired hamsters are shown on a bed of shavings in the UK, while longhaired hamsters are shown on wood-based cat litter. The wood-based cat litter allows even a very longhaired male to emerge for judging without long curlers of shavings matting his coat. Unlike some other animal fancies, the UK and US hamster fancies do not allow hamsters to be groomed once they have been benched. The US, and many other countries, also follow UK traditions when it comes to choice of bedding and show pens.

In addition to shavings or cat litter, some clubs insist that a piece of vegetable or fruit is present in the pens. This is to provide moisture for the hamster while it is contained in the show pen. In hot weather, most exhibitors choose a vegetable in preference to fruit, to avoid attracting wasps and insects. Some clubs may also allow a natural-coloured dog biscuit in the pen. Dog biscuits are chosen in preference to hamster food because the hamster cannot place a dog biscuit in its pouches as easily as normal hamster mix. Many hamsters will try to fill their pouches with hamster food if it is present, which makes it extremely difficult – if not impossible – for the judge to evaluate the hamster.

165

JUDGING

Once the hamsters have been placed in their pens and lined up in the judging square, judging will begin. The judge will remove a hamster from its pen and place it onto a judging frame. The frame has a wire-mesh insert, which allows the underneath of the hamster to be seen so that the judge can assess the condition of the belly fur, etc.

Hamster judging is tactile. The judge will stroke the hamster to feel the softness and thickness of fur, the condition of the hamster, and its size. It is not unusual for a seemingly large hamster with lots of fur to have a lightweight frame that could do with filling out! Running the hand over the hamster will also find any abnormality in the hamster's back, and the judges may also check the tail for any kinks.

MARKING CRITERIA

A judge will spend at least two years training, following the criteria laid down by the individual clubs. Marking may differ slightly from club to club, but the basic principles will be very similar. Normally, marks are given out of 100. The perfect hamster could gain 100 marks, but the nearest we have seen is 93.

Marks can be deducted as well as awarded. Exhibition Standard rules include penalties, which range from mandatory disqualification to a deduction of points. A hamster with a totally missing limb, or ear, or eye, or foot, or tail, would be disqualified, as would a sick, diseased, or intractable hamster (e.g. one that bites or cannot be controlled). A nick in the ear would possibly lose a hamster a point or so, as would a cut, a badly rubbed nose or excess fat!

The judge can also deduct marks for a poorly presented or dirty pen. As we were told by a gentleman who had kept hamsters since their introduction to the UK, *"If you have a beautiful animal, it is up to you to present it to the judge in an immaculate condition, which includes the container"*.

In the UK, which has a marking system out of 100, the marks for each section are approximately as follows.

Category	Potential Maximum
• Colour and markings	30
• Type	25
• Fur	20
• Size	10
• Condition	10
• Ears and eyes	5

(Other countries follow the same marking systems, although there may be minor differences in the allocation of points per category. Your local club will be able to answer any questions about marking criteria.)

Colour and markings: This category normally has the highest number of marks, to discourage indiscriminate breeding that would not only dilute many existing colours, but may also irretrievably damage the gene pool of hamsters. Your hamster will judged against the ideal described in the Standard for that colour. It is surprising how many shades there can be of a colour, even White! The length of hair will influence the marks for Colour and Markings; for example, a very longhaired male will look slightly paler than his shorthaired counterpart. This is because they have the same amount of colour in each hair but in the longhaired hamster it is spread over a much longer length of hair.

Type: Giving the Type category the second-highest allocation of marks helps to ensure that breeders strive to maintain the body type of the ideal hamster. The body should be broad and cobby. The head should be large in proportion to the body, with a broad skull, a short face, and a blunt nose. The overall profile should be Romanesque.

Fur: Fur should be soft and dense, including the belly fur. A remark frequently recorded by judges is "TBF", which means that the hamster has Thin Belly Fur! Longhaired males should have thick, dense long hair, but longhaired females should not lose any marks for not having the long, flowing hair of the males.

Size: Allowances will be made for the fact that females, in general, are larger than males. However, this does not mean that excess fat is acceptable. The judge is entitled to deduct marks for this.

Condition: The judge will check for dry skin on the ears or body, greasy fur, long toenails, overgrown teeth, or anything pertaining to the health of the hamster.

Ears and eyes: This mark is usually calculated by deducting points from the total available for any faults found. This can be for nicks in ears, crumpled ears, runny or closed eyes, or failing to hold the ears erect.

AFTER JUDGING

After each class has been judged and each hamster given its mark (written on the pen label by the book steward or the judge), the results are collated and sent to the show secretary. The book steward has the unenviable task of recording all these. In the UK, all these records are normally available to exhibitors, so that they can see where there are areas for improvement. In the US, the two main hamster clubs have adopted the UK rules virtually unchanged. In Norway and Sweden, judging is arranged so that exhibitors can hear what the judge has to say about each hamster.

Once judged, the pen stewards arrange the hamsters in points order on the show benches in readiness for the Duplicate classes. The hamsters are not judged a second time; instead a winner is chosen from the top-scoring hamsters of the various Straight classes. The winner is the hamster with the most points out of the potential 100. If any of the top-scoring hamsters have the same number of points, and they have not been judged against each other previously in the show, they will be separated (usually by giving a plus or minus mark) by the judge. At the end of judging, the hamster with the highest mark is awarded the title of Best In Show.

6. THE DWARF (OR OTHER SPECIES) SECTION

To enter hamsters in this section, you must follow the same entry procedure described in the section on Syrians. Full details of the Straight and Duplicate Classes can be found on the show schedule.
If you are in any doubt about which class your hamster is eligible to enter, check with the show secretary. If your hamster is one of the newer colours, double-check with a fellow Other Species exhibitor prior to benching. It is possible that the show secretary of the day does not keep Other Species and may not be aware which colours have a Standard and which do not.

In the UK and the US, the show pens for Other Species are different from the show pens for Syrians. Some clubs will allow exhibitors to use a Syrian show pen if no Other Species show pens are available, but you will need to check this prior to the show day. In other countries, a small plastic tank is used as a show pen.

The rules about bedding material and food, which are described in the Syrian section, also apply to the Other Species section, with one exception – as there are no longhaired Dwarfs all the exhibits are shown on shavings.

MORE THAN ONE?

As Dwarf and Chinese hamsters are normally kept in pairs or colonies, the rule of one animal per pen does not apply. Most clubs allow two animals (of the same species) per pen. If you have a pair, but only one of the hamsters is going to be entered into the show, you can take both to the show and place them in the same pen, provided that you inform the show secretary which hamster is to be judged. If you own a pair, and each hamster is being entered into a separate class, you will need to check the club rules, which can vary on this issue.

If the same pen holds two animals being shown in two different Straight classes – for example, if one is a Standard colour and one Non-Standard – the judge will not put an identifying note on the pen label as it is clear which animal is which. However, should the animals be entered in the same Straight class, the judge will need to know which mark belongs to which animal. If the hamsters are a mixed-sex pair, the pen labels will have 'male' or 'female' written on them, the symbols ♂ or ♀, or the initials M or F. Where the hamsters are of the same sex, a cryptic note may be noticed on the pen label, such as 'bigger', 'lighter', or 'bigger eyes', etc. This is simply so that the judge, and later the exhibitor, can tell which mark belongs to which animal.

Having two animals per pen can also make the pen steward's life a little more fraught. After judging has finished, the pens cannot be put into a strict points order. However, it is surprising how quickly pen stewards get adept at keeping track of where each animal slots into the marking.

JUDGING

The three species of hamster (Campbell, Winter White and Chinese) shown in the Other Species section are judged according to their different Standards. Non-Standard hamsters in the Other Species section usually consist of Non-Standard Campbells, as colour mutations in the Winter White and Chinese species all have Standards. There are now so many new Standard colours among the Campbell variety that some clubs have two or more classes to reduce the numbers per class.

The judging takes place in the same way as the judging of Syrians, with judging being tactile-based. Touching and stroking the hamster will establish its general condition, the thickness of its fur and any abnormalities in the spine, etc. Due to the smaller size of hamsters in the Other Species section, it is sometimes more difficult for a judge to examine certain features, such as toenails, sex, or a suspected abnormality. Therefore, a hamster may be 'scruffed', which means the judge holds the hamster by the scruff of its neck.

MARKING CRITERIA

Marking follows the same format described in the Syrian section, with the total number of points potentially being 100. As with Syrian hamsters, marks may be deducted as well as awarded. Under exhibition Standard rules, faults leading to mandatory disqualification include a missing limb, eye, foot, or ear, or a spinal deformity, as well as any hamster the judge considers to be sick, diseased, or in an advanced stage of pregnancy. Any hamster that is totally intractable (cannot be handled) at the time of judging could also be disqualified.

In the UK, which has a marking system out of 100, the marks for each section are approximately as follows.

Category	Potential Maximum
• Colour and markings	30
• Type	25
• Fur	20
• Size	10
• Condition	10
• Ears and eyes	5

Colour and markings: Each species is judged against the 'ideal' of that species, as described in the Standard. Patterned animals should conform where colour is present (e.g. eye colour, fur colour, etc.), but in some cases lighter-coloured patches may be permitted on the ears. Satin Campbells are judged according to the colour of their Standard with allowances being made for the effect of satinisation. Winter White hamsters showing signs of a winter coat would be heavily penalised under normal circumstances, as the Standard for a Winter White describes the summer coat. Albino Campbells and Pearl Winter Whites should be free from staining, which would also be penalised heavily.

Type: The 'ideal' laid down in the Standard for each species is used as a benchmark by the judge when allocating Type marks.

Fur: This includes the density, length, and quality of the fur on the whole of the body, including the feet, and, in the case of the Campbell and the Winter White, the ears.

Size: The ideal size is described in the Standard, and the judge will measure each hamster against this.

Condition: The hamster should be fit, curious when awake, and in a good condition for handling. Thin or overweight hamsters could lose some marks in this section, as would a female who had not come back into condition after rearing a litter.

Eyes and ears: Points would be deducted for runny, bulging or closed eyes, nicks in the ears, or ears that show evidence of having been recently bitten or damaged in any way.

AFTER JUDGING
The judge may be approached at the end of the show to discuss any decisions he or she has made. Always remember, however, that the judge's decision is final.

APPENDICES
USEFUL CONTACTS

1. UK hamster organisations
2. British, European and American hamster organisations
3. Genealogy w/ebsites

1. UK HAMSTER ORGANISATIONS

UK

National Hamster Council (NHC)
P.O.Box 154
Rotherham
South Yorkshire
S66 0FL

Website: http://www.hamsters-uk.org
E-mail: hamstercouncil@bigfoot.com

British Hamster Association (BHA)
P.O.Box 825
Sheffield
S17 3RU

Website: http://www.forrestg.pwp.blueyonder.co.uk/bha/

2. BRITISH, EUROPEAN, AMERICAN AND CANADIAN HAMSTER ORGANISATIONS

Heart of England Hamster Club (affiliated to BHA)
24 Huntercombe Lane North
Taplow
Maidenhead
SL6 0LG

Website: http://www.petwebsite.com/hoehc.htm
E-mail: flordon@aol.com

Midland Hamster Club (affiliated to NHC)
See National Hamster Council address, page 170.

Website: http://www.midlandhamsterclub.co.uk
E-mail: webmaster@midlandhamsterclub.co.uk

Northern Hamster Club (affiliated to NHC)
See National Hamster Council address, page 170.

Telephone: 01904 413426
Website: http://www.hamsterpage.ic24.net
E-mail: Sandra.n.h.c@ic24.net

Northern Ireland Hamster Club
4 Rusheyhill Road
Lisburn
County Antrim
BT28 3TD

Website: http://www.nihc.org.uk
E-mail: secretary@nihc.org.uk

Peter and Christine Logsdail (Towy Vale Hamstery)
25, High Street
Llandovey
Carmarthenshire
SA20 0PU

Telephone: 01550 720127
Website: http://www.hamster.hamm.org
E-mail: hamster@hamm.org

South of England Hamster Club
See National Hamster Council address, page 170.

Telephone: 01865 376686
Website: http://www.angelfire.com/ok/soehc
E-mail: parusater@btinternet.com

Appendix I

Southern Hamster Club
42 Stonebridge Drive
Frome
Somerset
BA11 2TN

Website:
http://www.somershire.freeserve.co.uk/southernhamsterclub/index.html.htm
E-mail: hamsters@somershire.freeserve.co.uk

The Hamster Society
3 Laverockdale Loan
Edinburgh
EH13 0EZ

Website: http://www.forrestg.pwp.blueyonder.co.uk/hamsoc/
E-mail: grant@hamsoc.org.uk

EUROPE

Danish Hamster Owners' Club
c/o Kenneth Worm
Staerevej 56
DK-2400 NV
Denmark

Website: http://www.hamsterland.dk
E-mail: info@hamsterland.dk

Finnish Hamster Club (Suomen Hamsteriyhdistys Ry)
Website: http://www.hamsteriyhdistys.net
E-mail: wenmaster@hamsteriyhdistys.net

Netherlands Hamster Club
Poptahof Zuid 627
2624 SN Delft
Netherlands

Website: http://www.exotics.nl
E-mail: t.c.van.der.ende@exotics.nl

Swedish Hamster Foundation (Svenska Hamsterforeningen)
c/o Parkgatan 10
S-592 32 Vadstena
Sweden

Website: http://www.algonet.se/~hamster/shf.htm
E-mail: hamster@algonet.se

USA

American Hamster Association (AHA)
PO Box 457
Leavenworth
Kansas 66048

Website: http://www.hamsterclub.org
E-mail: info@hamsterclub.org

California Hamster Assocation
23651 Dune Mear
Lake Forest
California 92630

Website: http://www.geocities.com/CalHamAssoc
E-mail: calhamassoc@hotmail.com

Pioneer Rat and Hamster Society (PRHS)
PO Box 10624
Kansas City
Missouri 64188-0624

Website: http://www.prhs.info
E-mail: prhs@prhs.info

Rat, Mouse and Hamster Fanciers' Association
783 Solana Drive
Lafayette
California 94549

Website: http://www.ratmousehamster.com/rmhf/rmhf.htm
E-mail: jstarkey@telis.org

CANADA

Ontario Hamster Club
2891 Lakeshore Road
Bright's Grove
Ontario
N0N 1C0
Email: bkershaw@ebtech.net

3. GENEALOGY WEBSITES

Breeders' Assistant for Hamsters
Website: http://www.tenset.co.uk/ba/hamster/index.html
E-mail: ba-hamsters@tenset.co.uk

Appendix I

I-Breed Pedigree and Livestock Management System
Website: http://www.ibreed.ukgateway.net
E-mail: iBreed@ukgateway.net

Laotzu's Animal Register
Website: http://animalregister.net
E-mail: enquiries@animalregister.net

Pedigrees 2000
Website: http://www.pedigrees2000.com
E-mail: wruther@702com.net

Zoo Easy
Website: www.zooeasy.com
E-mail: support@zooeasy.com